Bloom's

GUIDES

Ralph Ellison's

Invisible Man

CURRENTLY AVAILABLE

The Adventures of Huckleberry Finn
All the Pretty Horses
Animal Farm
The Autobiography of Malcolm X
The Awakening
Beloved
Beowulf
Brave New World
The Canterbury Tales
The Catcher in the Rye
The Chosen
The Crucible
Cry, the Beloved Country
Death of a Salesman
Fahrenheit 451
Frankenstein
The Glass Menagerie
The Grapes of Wrath
Great Expectations
The Great Gatsby
Hamlet
The Handmaid's Tale
The House on Mango Street
I Know Why the Caged Bird Sings
The Iliad
Invisible Man
Jane Eyre
Lord of the Flies
Macbeth
Maggie: A Girl of the Streets
The Member of the Wedding
The Metamorphosis
Native Son
1984
The Odyssey
Oedipus Rex
Of Mice and Men
One Hundred Years of Solitude
Pride and Prejudice
Ragtime
The Red Badge of Courage
Romeo and Juliet
The Scarlet Letter
A Separate Peace
Slaughterhouse-Five
Snow Falling on Cedars
The Stranger
A Streetcar Named Desire
The Sun Also Rises
A Tale of Two Cities
The Things They Carried
To Kill a Mockingbird
Uncle Tom's Cabin
The Waste Land
Wuthering Heights

Bloom's
GUIDES

Ralph Ellison's
Invisible Man

Edited & with an Introduction
by Harold Bloom

BLOOM'S LITERARY CRITICISM
An imprint of Infobase Publishing

Bloom's Guides: Invisible Man

Bloom's Literary Criticism
An imprint of Infobase Publishing
132 West 31st Street
New York, NY 10001

Library of Congress Cataloging-in-Publication Data
Ralph Ellison's Invisible man / [edited by] Harold Bloom.
p. cm. — (Bloom's guides)
Includes bibliographical references and index.
ISBN 978-0-7910-9790-8 (hardcover)
1. Ellison, Ralph. Invisible man. 2. African American men in literature. 3. African Americans in literature. I. Bloom, Harold. II. Title. III. Series.

PS3555.L625I5363 2008
813'.54—dc22

2007036553

Bloom's Literary Criticism books are available at special discounts when purchased in bulk quantities for businesses, associations, institutions, or sales promotions. Please call our Special Sales Department in New York at (212) 967-8800 or (800) 322-8755.

You can find Bloom's Literary Criticism on the World Wide Web at http://www.chelseahouse.com

Contributing Editor: Portia Williams Weiskel

Cover design by Takeshi Takahashi

Printed in the United States of America

Bang EJB 10 9 8 7 6 5 4 3 2 1

This book is printed on acid-free paper.

Contents

Introduction

HAROLD BLOOM

1

I have argued elsewhere that the late Ralph Waldo Ellison's *Invisible Man* represents the outstanding African American achievement in the arts to date, except for the musical accomplishments of Louis Armstrong, Charlie Parker, and Bud Powell. At once comic and tragic, and alas still prophetic, *Invisible Man* competes with the work of Thomas Pynchon and Philip Roth as the most distinguished American prose fiction since the death of William Faulkner. The imaginative wealth of Ellison's only published novel seems inexhaustible; fresh insights become apparent with each rereading. At once naturalistic, Impressionist-symbolic, and surrealistic, the book ends in a mode of irrealism, pioneering a style exploited by Pynchon in *Gravity's Rainbow*. Like his namesake Emerson, Ellison was both a transcendentalist and a pragmatist, and again like Emerson, he firmly resisted the apocalyptic temptation. Fleeing both the Brotherhood (the Communist Party) and Ras the Exhorter (a forerunner of the younger Malcolm X and Farrakhan), the Invisible Man goes underground, to cultivate an ultimate self-reliance, illuminated by 1,369 old-fashioned filament lightbulbs, which he enjoys while refusing to pay tribute to Monopolated Light & Power (Consolidated Edison).

The African-American critic Robert B. Stepto has identified in Ellison's novel, as elsewhere in black fiction, "the narratives of ascent and immersion." In Douglas Robinson's development of these movements, they come together as "the Jonah motif." Following Father Mapple's great sermon on Jonah in Melville's *Moby-Dick*, Ellison has his Invisible Man listen to a record of Louis Armstrong, greatest genius of jazz, singing and playing "What Did I Do to Be So Black and Blue." Within Armstrong's music, in a visionary breakthrough, Ellison's hero hears another music, in which a preacher and congregation exchange answers, and the preacher cries out: "It'll put you, glory, glory, Oh my Lawd, in the WHALE'S BELLY." Jonah, a failed prophet, is also a survivor, and so is the nameless Invisible Man, Ellison's equivalent of Melville's Ishmael, the narrator of *Moby-Dick*. Weary of being a phantom in the mind of other people, white *and* black, the Invisible Man survives underground in the whale's belly, augmenting his sense of self and perfecting an image of voice that can speak universally.

Ellison was a great artist, not a social activist, and he suffered much abuse from those who felt he was not revolutionary or separatist enough. He wisely declined to compromise his mastery of the art of fiction by becoming the novelist version either of Ras the Exhorter, wholehearted but doom-eager, or the sinister Rinehart, reverend and runner, both of whom have their mock-aesthetic equivalents. T. S. Eliot and Joseph Conrad mattered greatly to his writing, and so did Louis Armstrong and Charlie Parker. The humor, the pathos, the invention of *Invisible Man* manifest themselves upon the highest level of American fiction. Lurking in the book, underground with its protagonist, is a tragedy, not so much of the African Americans but of most Americans of good will, of whatever lineage. Call it the social tragedy of the United States of America, already two nations if not more, and being driven toward despair and violence by the emancipation of selfishness that belongs to the political age.

2

Invisible Man is more than a century old, and reads as freshly and strongly today as it ever did. Most American novels of the second half of our century are already period pieces; very few have joined the major works of Dreiser, Faulkner, Hemingway, Fitzgerald, and Cather as classic American fictions. *Invisible Man* is indisputably one of those few, together with Thomas Pynchon's *The Crying of Lot 49* and *Gravity's Rainbow*, Cormac McCarthy's *Blood Meridian*, Don DeLillo's massive *Underworld*, Vladimir Nabokov's *Pale Fire*, Philip Roth's *Zuckerman Bound*, and one or two others. There is an intensity and vividness throughout *Invisible Man* that allies it to Faulkner's *As I Lay Dying* and Nathanael West's *Miss Lonelyhearts.* Faulkner in particular is Ellison's prime American precursor, as he is also for Toni Morrison, the principal African American novelist since Ellison. Like Faulkner, Ellison had a stylistic debt to Joyce. There is also a Kafkan strand to *Invisible Man*, particularly evident in the novel's irrealistic elements, including its curious comic effects. For all this, *Invisible Man* remains a refreshingly original work, carefully controlling its biblical allusions (particularly to the Book of Jonah) and its stance in relation to previous American fiction, from Melville through Mark Twain to Faulkner.

Invisible Man is astonishingly rich in its textures, overtones, and undersongs; in a profound sense it is akin to jazz, the African-American art in which Ellison was profoundly immersed. Berndt Ostendorf, a German scholar both of jazz history and of African American literature, subtly finds Ellison's structural and thematic reliance upon jazz to be the novelist's attempt to reconcile his high aesthetic modernism with African American folk culture. The greatest figures in jazz tradition—Louis Armstrong and Charlie Parker—mediate T.S. Eliot, Joyce, Faulkner, and Kafka for Ellison. A novelist born in Oklahoma City in 1914 necessarily became aware of American literature from Emerson through Eliot, and as an African American similarly developed an early awareness that jazz was the uniquely American art form, blending an African base with European influences much as Walt Whitman fused the American languages with Western poetic and prophetic tradition. Ostendorf, in my judgment, joins the late Kenneth Burke as Ellison's most useful critic to date. Burke, the finest American critic since Emerson, emphasized that *Invisible Man* constantly *remade its epoch*, and never merely reflected the age. The truth of Burke's insight is reaffirmed by Ostendorf's tactful account of African American nationalist resistance to Ellison's achievement. No one who knew Ellison could fail to be aware of his scorn for mindlessness, whether it emanated from whites or blacks, past or present. The aesthetic eminence of *Invisible Man* isolated Ellison, who nevertheless refused Richard Wright's and James Baldwin's self-exiles, and remained in a country where he suffered the experience of having many more white than African-American admirers. He once told me that he sadly agreed with my melancholy conclusion that the poetry of Langston Hughes was overesteemed, but also chided me for admiring Zora Neale Hurston's *Their Eyes Were Watching God*, which he judged to be more improvised than written. A critical stance as uncompromising as Ellison's cost him a great deal, and certainly was one of the factors that kept him from publishing a second major novel in his lifetime. Ellison was highly conscious that he had joined Armstrong and Parker as an artist of the highest order, and he refused to descend below that extraordinary eminence.

It is difficult to reread *Invisible Man* without experiencing a sadness that in one sense is wholly external to the novel's exuberance, since the nameless narrator prophesies for himself a world of "infinite possibilities":

> Yes, but what *is* the next phase? How often have I tried to find it! Over and over again I've gone up above to seek it out. For, like almost everyone else in our country, I started out with my share of optimism. I believed in hard work and progress and action, but now, after first being "for" society and then "against" it, I assign myself no rank or any limit, and such an attitude is very much against the trend of the times. But my world has become one of infinite possibilities. What a phrase—still it's a good phrase and a good view of life, and a man shouldn't accept any other; that much I've learned underground. Until some gang succeeds in putting the world in a strait-jacket, its definition is possibility. Step outside the narrow borders of what men call reality and you step into chaos—ask Rinehart, he's a master of it—or imagination. That too I've learned in the cellar, and not by deadening my sense of perception; I'm invisible, not blind.

The choice of stepping into chaos *or* imagination is Emersonian, even if, as an African American, Ellison sometimes was rueful about bearing Emerson's name. The Invisible Man indeed is a black Emersonian, which is a difference that makes a difference, but still has more in common with Emerson, than with T.S. Eliot or with Faulkner, or any other white American precursor. Emerson, when most himself, wrote as a universalist. Since his chief work was his endless journal, he did not always refrain from self-contradiction, but Ellison has a shrewd sense of what was deepest in Emerson, as did W.E.B. Du Bois, who quarried from the Sage of Concord his fecund but dark sense of "double consciousness." *The Souls of Black Folk* seems to me to have the same relation to Emerson that *Invisible Man* achieves. Du Bois and Ellison transform Emerson just as Whitman and Dickinson did; they transumptively triumph by making Emerson black, even as Whitman and Dickinson extended Emerson to poetic ends that sometimes fulfilled his implicit criteria, and sometimes reversed him, Whitman by an Epicurean materialism, and Dickinson by a skepticism so nihilistic as to go beyond even the abyss-worship of "Fate" in *The Conduct of Life*. Ellison, like Du Bois, became more Emersonian than Emerson himself had been, once his earliest, most antinomian phase was over. Du Bois translated an Emersonian asset into a dialectical burden, and Du Bois's disciples have retranslated that burden into a pained and painful opportunity. Ellison's ironies can be sublimely difficult, and they make even contradictory reading of "infinite possibilities" equally possible. What Emerson himself called "the cost of confirmation" was tragically high for Ellison, but it gave him, and anyone capable of authentic reading, a great novel.

Biographical Sketch

Ralph Waldo Ellison was born on March 1, 1914, in Oklahoma City, Oklahoma. His father, Lewis Ellison, was a construction worker and tradesman who died when Ellison was three. His mother, Ida Millsap, worked as a domestic servant but was active in radical politics for many years. Ellison thrived on the discarded magazines and phonograph records she brought home from the white households where she worked. He attended Douglass High School in Oklahoma City, where he learned the soprano saxophone, trumpet, and other instruments, playing both jazz and light classical music.

In 1933 Ellison began studying music at the Tuskegee Institute in Alabama. He remained there for three years before going to New York in 1936, where he held a number of odd jobs while continuing to study music and sculpture. In New York he met Langston Hughes and Richard Wright, who gave him great encouragement in his writing. Ellison's short stories, essays, and reviews began appearing in the *Antioch Review*, the *New Masses*, and many other magazines and journals in the late 1930s. At this time his interest in social justice attracted him to the Communist Party, although he would later repudiate it. Ellison gained a modicum of financial security in 1938 when he was hired by the Federal Writers' Project to gather folklore and present it in literary form. The four years he spent at this work enriched his own writing by providing source material that would be incorporated into his own fiction.

In 1943, wishing to help in the war effort, Ellison joined the merchant marine. The next year he received a Rosenwald Foundation Fellowship to write a novel; although he mapped out a plot, he failed to finish the work (one section was published as a short story, "Flying Home"). After the war he went to a friend's farm in Vermont to recuperate, and it was here that he conceived the novel that would establish him as a major writer—*Invisible Man*. He worked on the book for five years, and it was finally published in 1952. This long novel is both a historical biography of the black man in America and an allegory of man's quest for identity. *Invisible Man* received the National Book Award for fiction in 1953 and is now regarded as one of the most distinguished American novels of the century. *Shadow and Act* (1964), Ellison's second book, is a collection of personal essays about literature, folklore, jazz, and the author's life.

Even before finishing *Invisible Man*, Ellison had conceived the idea for another novel. Although he published several segments of it as short stories and read others on television and at lectures, the work remained unfinished at the time of his death; a large portion of it was destroyed by a fire at Ellison's summer home in Massachusetts in 1967. Because he did not advocate black separatism, Ellison fell out of sympathy with the black writers and thinkers of the 1960s; but over the last two decades he again became a much sought-after lecturer on college campuses. A second collection of essays, *Going to the Territory*, was published in 1986.

Ralph Ellison held a fellowship of the American Academy of Arts and Letters in Rome from 1955 to 1957 and received the United States Medal of Freedom in 1969. He held visiting professorships at Yale, Bard College, the University of Chicago, and elsewhere. From 1970 to 1979 he was Albert Schweitzer Professor in the Humanities at New York University, later becoming an emeritus professor there. He was a charter member of the National Council of the Arts, served as trustee of the John F. Kennedy Center for the Performing Arts, and was honorary consultant in American Letters at the Library of Congress. Ellison was married twice, but details of his first marriage are unavailable; in 1946 he married Fanny McConnell. Ralph Ellison died in New York City on April 16, 1994.

The Story Behind the Story

The *Introduction to the Science of Sociology*, Park and Burgess's standard textbook for college sociology classes in the 1930s, offers this definition: "The Negro is, by natural disposition, neither an intellectual nor an idealist, like the Jew; nor a brooding introspective, like the East Indian; nor a pioneer and frontiersman, like the Anglo-Saxon. He is primarily an artist, loving life for its own sake. His métier is expression rather than action. He is, so to speak, the lady among the races" (quoted in Ellison, *Shadow and Act*, 1964, pp. 25–26). Nothing less than America's own racial history is the story behind the story of *Invisible Man*, but it is not sufficient to explain the entire measure of both impact and controversy associated—now and at the time of publication (1952)—with Ralph Ellison's novel.

The diversity of influences begins with Ellison's name and place of birth. From a grandfather born into slavery (1837) came a father, Lewis Ellison (1877), who witnessed a lynching at age five, and who became sufficiently literate and optimistic to name his own son at birth (1913) after Ralph Waldo Emerson, the distinguished, white, American renaissance man, famous for essays and orations espousing self-reliance and the force of character. This naming of Ellison reflected a father's hope that his son's life would not be constrained by the color of his skin and would by its own virtue and power advance the standing of the black race in America. In turn, Ellison's later-in-life controversial and transformative decision (and that of his famous protagonist's) to break free from possessive ideologies reflects the wide reach of early influences. Wrestling, as Ellison and his protagonist do, with the sometimes-liberating, sometimes-paralyzing divisions within the self is a consequence of reflection and studied self-awareness and another example of early "messages" played out in life and fiction. The influences of Ellison's mother were more overt. An activist supporter of racial justice and Eugene Debs's Socialist Party, Ida Ellison instructed her sons to "do something" to help the "Negro race" (Jackson 8). Urgency about race relations in America was thus potently internalized in Ellison's notion of personal destiny.

As a place of birth and childhood, Oklahoma—a rogue state of sorts, Southern in geography, but not slaveholding—gave mixed messages to the young Ellison. Its wide open spaces kept alive the frontier spirit of adventure and self-resourcefulness and tolerated the coexistence of whites, blacks, and American Indians. Jim Crow laws, however, segregated Oklahoma City's facilities including schools where "separate" almost never meant "equal." Ellison's education—through neighborhood mentors and storytellers, a large library in the church-owned home rented by the Ellison family, and a few unusually talented teachers in his school—was substantial and varied. Especially rich was his extensive music education. Ellison entered Tuskegee Institute at nineteen intending to study music and write a symphony to celebrate his extensive experiences. These biographical details speak to the confidence and eclectic spirit—uncommon for a black man raised in poverty in Ellison's generation—that made possible the concept of "Invisible Man" and Ellison's achievement—powerful and still in dispute—in American race relations and literature.

Published in April 1952, *Invisible Man* "burst upon the American scene," in the words of Ellison critic, John Callahan, "with the combustion of a prairie fire accelerating across the open country of Oklahoma . . ." (*Ralph Ellison's "Invisible Man": A Casebook* 293). Years later, Norman Mailer likened his reading of Ellison to "holding a live electric wire in one's hand" (*Advertisements for Myself*, 1981, 432).

Although based at a Tuskegee-like college in the South and in the streets and tenements of New York City's Harlem in the 1920s and 1930s, the novel's famous first sentence—"I am an invisible man"—came to Ellison in a Waitsfield, Vermont, barn where—at a friend's invitation—Ellison had in 1945 secluded himself to write and regain his health. The concept of "invisibility" was a striking and timely device for dramatizing the plight of black people in America in the long decades before *Brown* v. *Board of Education* rendered unconstitutional the "separate but equal" segregation ruling of *Plessy* v. *Ferguson* (1896). Under Jim Crow laws white people could avoid *seeing* black people, who, in turn, responded with quiet despair or seething anger to the intractable obstructions and deprivations they encountered on a daily basis. Ellison's novel forced a mutual and new "seeing" and dramatized different manifestations of the despair and seething anger. Before its publication no major American writer had focused so intimately and thoroughly on the psychological and cultural life of black Americans.

These features of the novel combined with the moment in history of its publication—the early days of what would become the lengthy, still-incomplete, sometimes-brutal, sometimes stirring civil rights movement—made for an immediate commercial and artistic success. Prominent among the numerous awards bestowed following publication were the National Book Award and the Chicago Defender's Award for "symbolizing the best in American democracy"—both in 1953; the naming of *Invisible Man* by literary luminaries in 1965 as "the most distinguished work of the past twenty years"; and the granting to Ellison by President Lyndon B. Johnson of the Medal of Freedom in 1969. Numerous honorary degrees from Harvard, Tuskegee, Williams, and other prestigious institutions and visiting professorships from all over reflected the widespread esteem *Invisible Man* had earned for Ellison. It has been translated into more than twenty languages.

Critical readers of *Invisible Man* have discerned in it an astonishing number and range of influences. The wide reading Ellison did as a youth is everywhere apparent. A random selection of these influences includes the word *spook* in the first paragraph, a bold choice because of its negative connotation for black people and a connection to Edgar Allan Poe and the American Spiritualist movement; the multilayered references connecting the theme of running, from old Negro slavery songs, with the dream warning from his grandfather ("Keep this Nigger-Boy Running") and the words of betrayal in Bledsoe's letter ("Please . . . keep [this Robin] running") with the grim poem depicting the victimization of poor Robin by "picking [him] clean [of] all the feathers"; the similarity of Invisible

Man's opening sentence to Ishmael's "Call me Ishmael" in Melville's *Moby-Dick*; the ancient theme of journey and descent (flight from South to North, rural to urban, work in the boiler room, falling into manhole) reminiscent of Aeneas, Dante, Orestes, Ulysses of Homer and Leopold Bloom of Joyce, the biblical Jonah, and Dostoyevsky's Underground Man; the Whitman-like tone evoking memories of Ellison's college ("Oh long green stretch of campus, Oh, quiet songs at dusk. . . ."); jazz and the blues ("What did I do to be so black and blue?"); the Brer Rabbit tales; and the similarity of Mark Antony's lines from Shakespeare's *Julius Caesar* ("My heart is in the coffin there with Caesar") and Invisible Man's eulogy at Tod Clifton's funeral ("He's in the box and we're in there with him"). Ellison was especially fascinated with T.S. Eliot and undertook the task of researching and understanding all the myriad references in *The Waste Land*. The experience inspired him to replicate a similar density of meaning in his own work. An exhaustive list of influences in *Invisible Man* is not possible. Some critics have made them the focus of their research (see especially Sundquist, *Cultural Contexts for Ralph Ellison's "Invisible Man,"* 1995, and Jackson, *Ralph Ellison: Emergence of Genius*, 2002).

A full appreciation of *Invisible Man* is not possible without knowledge of the intoxicating and strident political temper of Ellison's times. New York was the center of activity, and, with the encouragement of Richard Wright, a published black writer, Ellison gravitated to the intellectual and political left which included the Communist Party of America. The party's revolutionary optimism and support for the oppressed held a natural appeal for Ellison in particular and blacks longsuffering under the prevailing discriminatory practices in general. Moreover, the genuine absence of prejudice in the party and its readiness to encourage and publish black writers was gratifyingly useful to Ellison. When the difference between the desire to overthrow the system (Marxist class struggle) and the desire to reform, join, and gain power in the existing system (the accommodation supported by moderates) became clear, however, Ellison and the party parted company. In fact, the party was among the first to attack Ellison after the release of *Invisible Man* for not emphasizing the class aspects of black subjugation. But the novel generated hostility toward Ellison from a different faction within the black community. John Killems, reviewer for the leftist newspaper *Freedom*, blasted Ellison for denigrating black life with stereotypical figures and tawdry images: "The Negro people need . . . *Invisible Man* like we need . . . a stab in the back" (quoted in Neal, "Ellison's Zoot Suit," *Twentieth Century Views*, 1974, 63). Members of the incipient Black Separatist Movement attacked Ellison for his perceived posture of accommodation.

These issues come to life in the characters of Jim Trueblood, Dr. Bledsoe, Tod Clifton, Brother Jack, and Ras the Exhorter (based loosely on Marcus Garvey, the Jamaican immigrant who, in the same time period, stood on ladders in Harlem exhorting black separatism and "Africa for the Africans" and founded Rastafarianism). The riot that concludes the novel is reminiscent of similarly inspired race riots in Detroit and Harlem.

Ellison responded quickly, emphatically, and often to these attacks. He insisted that his efforts to encourage the creation of personal consciousness which included drawing on and appropriating the richness of black experience in America was a more truly revolutionary act leading to a more sustainable version of freedom.

The debate has continued, expanded, and become more informed as well as recently updated (see two reviews of Arnold Rampersad's *Ralph Ellison: A Biography*, Knopf, 2007: Hilton Als, "A look at the life of Ralph Ellison," *The New Yorker*, May 7, 2007, pp. 74–80, and Michael Anderson, "At a Loss for Words," *The Nation*, May 28, 2007, pp. 11–18). The Cambridge Companion series has recently brought out an edition on Ellison praising him for being the American writer who "most forcefully took up the challenge of thinking beyond the imprisoning reductiveness of race and of liberating the cosmopolitan energies of democracy" (Ross Posnock, ed., *The Cambridge Companion to Ralph Ellison*, 2005, p. 1).

List of Characters

The **Invisible Man** is the rhetorically flamboyant unnamed narrator of Ellison's novel. He is invisible not because he is a "spook"—literally unseen—but because he is a black man living in the racist atmosphere of America in the 1920s and 1930s, unrecognized because of his skin color. The narrator's insistent, cadenced oratorical style sweeps the reader into his world as he looks back, from the seclusion of an underground coal cellar on the border of Harlem, on the past twenty years of his life. The narrator is an angry, embittered speaker who recalls, often with heavy sarcasm, his younger naive and hopeful self, both as a student at a black southern college and later as the Harlem District leader of a quasi-Communist movement in New York City. Like a classic picaresque hero, he falls unwittingly into a series of grotesque tragic-comic adventures that, with explosive violence, shatter his beliefs about race relations, the world, and his place in it.

Dr. Bledsoe is the president of the narrator's southern black college, an impressive paternal role model who nonetheless betrays the hero and expels him from the idyllic campus. His is a classic success story: he has risen from an illiterate boy to an influential spokesman for the race; he is a gracious, humble intermediary between the college and the white board of trustees; and he is the owner of two Cadillacs. When the narrator antagonizes one of the trustee members, he incurs the wrath of Dr. Bledsoe, who reveals both his true beliefs—"the only way to please a white man is to tell him a lie"—and the autocratic power with which he runs this seeming bastion of racial harmony.

Mr. Norton is the white northern college trustee whom the narrator unintentionally chauffeurs through a series of nightmarish incidents. In the process of meeting a black sharecropper, who has impregnated his own daughter, and witnessing a riot in a black bar and brothel, Mr. Norton is stripped of his illusions about the peaceful advancement of black society. He returns to the campus in shock.

Mr. Emerson, the son of one of the college trustees, interviews the narrator for a job and ends up showing him Dr. Bledsoe's damning sealed letter of introduction. He is a wealthy white patron of black art, who takes pity on this victim of Bledsoe's rage and tips him off to a job at the Liberty paint factory.

Mary is the motherly head of a boarding house in Harlem who takes in the narrator after his electroshock therapy at the paint factory's hospital. She offers him support during his months of unemployment, confident that he will eventually assist in the betterment of his race.

Brother Jack is one of the leaders of the clandestine "Brotherhood" in New York, a political movement that advocates the mobilization of the masses and scientific objectivity and that is clearly modeled on contemporary Communism. A sprightly red-haired man with a penetrating gaze, he selects the narrator as the new district leader for Harlem after seeing him lead a protest against an eviction. Brother Jack moves mysteriously between the swank parties of wealthy donors and the mass demonstrations of the underprivileged. He first defends the narrator against jealous party members but later sacrifices the Harlem District in a calculated play for propaganda.

Tod Clifton is another Brotherhood Harlem District leader, a strikingly handsome daredevil who fights with members from a rival movement and helps the narrator mobilize the community. His commitment to the Brotherhood is not absolute—he talks of the temptation to renounce ideology and "plunge out of history"—and when the narrator temporarily leaves Harlem, he disappears. The hero spots him several days later, selling demeaning black puppets on a street corner. When harassed by a policeman, Clifton resists and is shot. Clifton's funeral marks the narrator's real break from the Brotherhood: in the face of blatant racial violence he cannot bring himself to preach the objective ideological party line.

Ras the Exhorter is the narrator's political rival, the leader of a Harlem black separatist movement whose ornery henchmen regularly disrupt Brotherhood demonstrations. Based on the historical figure of Marcus Garvey, Ras represents the alternative to the narrator's political ideology: rejection both of whites and the principles of universal equality. When a race riot erupts in Harlem, Ras relishes the violence: dressed in African garb, he charges through the streets on horseback and hurls spears at the police and the narrator.

Rinehart is an elusive resident of Harlem who represents another alternative to the narrator's Brotherhood. The narrator first learns of him when, disguised in sunglasses and the wide-brimmed hat of a zoot-suiter, he is mistaken by several beautiful women for their protector. Rinehart is the ultimate con man, a corrupt minister, a gambler, and a pimp. The narrator briefly decides to imitate him, selfishly abusing his power to get back at the Brotherhood.

Sybil is the pampered wife of a white party leader whom the narrator, disillusioned by Clifton's death, uses for political purposes. She eagerly accepts his invitation home and, in the drunken flirtation that follows, reveals her ignorance of her husband's position and her predilection for interracial rape fantasies, casting the narrator as "Brother Taboo-with-whom-all-things-are-possible." She last appears on 110th Street, demanding to be taken to Harlem as the narrator loads her into a cab headed downtown.

Summary and Analysis

The title character of Ralph Ellison's *Invisible Man*, a novel about an unnamed young black man's political and racial self-discovery, admires Louis Armstrong's song "What Did I Do to Be So Black and Blue." In the **prologue**, he asks the same question about his own life, wondering at his fate as a black man in an indifferent racist society. The novel itself is structured like a jazz performance; the narrator adopts a fluid, improvisational voice and introduces themes in the prologue that run, elaborated and varied, throughout his story.

The setting of the prologue is surreal: the narrator, who has rejected society after years of hope and political involvement, lives on the border of Harlem in an underground room brilliantly lit by 1,369 light bulbs. The heat and electricity are pirated from Monopolated Light & Power, which, because of the speaker's "invisibility," cannot detect the source of the power drain. There are subversive advantages, the narrator comically implies, to going unseen in society. This invisibility clearly symbolizes the racism indigenous to America in the first half of the century—the speaker says he is unseen not because he is a "spook" but because "people refuse to see me . . . they see only my surroundings, themselves, or figments of their imagination." The narrator's comedy quickly mixes with rage as he recalls the constant affronts his imperceptibility has engendered. In one instance, an accidental jostle and automatic slur spurred him to demand an apology from a white passerby. Receiving instead only confused epithets, he beat and kicked the man, preparing even to cut his throat before he realized that the victim regarded the assault as terrifyingly unmotivated, "a walking nightmare." Stunned by his own inefficacy, the narrator burst out laughing and ran from the scene.

These often grotesque strains of comedy and violence, as well as the motifs of sight and blindness, darkness and light, recur throughout the book. Added to these are the themes of hallucinogenics, drunkenness, nightmares, music, and oratory, the powers of which the narrator also explores in the prologue.

Smoking marijuana and listening to Louis Armstrong, he leads the reader into the cultural "depths" of the music, hearing below the fast tempo a slower black spiritual, the call and response of a black congregation's sermon, and the laughter and tears of a slave woman whose master has died. The prologue ends with a reaffirmation of the narrator's belief in action and a defense of his phantom attacks on society's "dreamers and sleepwalkers," who refuse to perceive him.

The narrator then begins to tell his life history, in some ways an extended series of initiations into various institutions, each ending in betrayal, explosive violence, nightmarish perceptual distortion, and a loss of control. The first of these experiences takes place in **chapter one**, when the narrator, the high school valedictorian, is asked to give his speech on black humility as the "very essence of progress" to a gathering of his town's leading white citizens. The other entertainments are to be a boxing match or "battle royal" among nine black roughs and, the boys learn on entering the ballroom, a striptease. The narrator reacts with horror as the moral leaders of the community, drunk, force the black boys to stand in front of a naked blond dancer as she tantalizes them with her movements. The tempo of the dance music quickens, the white men begin to touch and chase her, and she narrowly escapes, leaving the traumatized black youths to go through with the fight. The narrator is forced to participate, and all ten youths are blindfolded and egged on with racial slurs in a crazed battle, which ends with the narrator getting knocked out. They are then urged to collect their prize money from a pile of cash strewn on a rug, which turns out to be electrically wired. Scrambling for coins, shoved and pushed by the drunken audience, they are repeatedly shocked with intolerable volts of electricity. Only after this wild manhandling is the narrator asked to give his valedictory address. Showing him weak, bloodied, yelling, and choking over the noise of the audience, Ellison depicts his hero's speech on racial harmony with heavy irony.

The performance nonetheless earns him a scholarship to a prestigious southern black college, an idyllic bastion of learning where he hopes to follow in the footsteps of the distinguished black president, Dr. Bledsoe (**chapter two**). But the speaker's dreams are shattered in the spring of his junior year when, during Founder's Day, he gets the job of chauffeuring one of the college's wealthy white trustees. Mr. Norton asks the narrator to drive into the countryside during a break between meetings, meanwhile lecturing him on his luck at being part of a "great dream become reality." Instead of showing him the sanitized, idealized version of black life in the South that Dr. Bledsoe would like him to see, the protagonist unintentionally drives Mr. Norton through an impoverished black area, thus, in the words of Dr. Bledsoe, "dragging the entire race into the slime!" Mr. Norton, first unaware of his surroundings, continues with a story about his beautiful daughter, "too pure for life," to whose memory he has dedicated his philanthropy. The trustee then notices a rundown shack—a former slave cottage—belonging to Jim Trueblood, a delinquent black sharecropper, and orders the car to stop. Here Mr. Norton learns with horror of Trueblood's incestuous relationship with his daughter, who, along with her mother, is visibly pregnant. Mr. Norton listens to the farmer with a mixture of horror and fascination, hearing the man's story of poverty, lust, nightmares, and violence. The effect on the white man is catastrophic; he appears on the verge of a stroke and, pleading for whiskey, orders the narrator to drive on.

As in so many of the narrator's misadventures, his well-intentioned decision, in this case to take Mr. Norton to the closest bar, the Golden Day, only leads to greater calamity. The Golden Day is a brothel to which a group of mentally ill black war veterans is taken once a week. In **chapter three** they have already arrived when the narrator brings his half-conscious charge inside. With the ironic clairvoyance of the insane, they recognize Mr. Norton as a Thomas Jefferson, a John D. Rockefeller, and even the Messiah. A riot breaks out almost immediately. Their supervisor, a giant black man named Supercargo, calls for order, but the veterans charge him, knocking him down and beating him unconscious. The narrator rescues Mr. Norton by taking him upstairs. He is greeted by prostitutes and a deranged former doctor who, after reviving the trustee, describes his wrongful treatment as a member of the medical profession. The doctor accuses the hero of delusional submission to white society and laughs scornfully at Mr. Norton's patronage of the college, driving the two back downstairs. Mr. Norton narrowly escapes the riotous crowd below and returns to campus in a state of shock.

Dr. Bledsoe's wrath falls on the narrator with unanticipated fervor (**chapter four**). Bledsoe tells him that he should have manipulated Mr. Norton: "We take these white folks where we want them to go, we show them what we want them to see." In a gesture emblematic of this maxim, Bledsoe composes his rage-distorted face to address the white trustee with humility and concern. The narrator then attends the proceedings of Founder's Day with guilt-ridden veneration, anticipating his expulsion.

Ellison's imagery in **chapter five**, describing the gathering students with "limbs stiff and voices now silent, as though on exhibit even in the dark, and the moon a white man's bloodshot eye," is typically vivid and surreal. The students sing black spirituals for the benefit of the visiting white patrons, and then the Reverend Homer A. Barbee gives a speech remembering the college's original black founder. In one of the striking examples of oratory that fill Ellison's novel, he passionately invokes the messianic life of the Founder—born a slave. The narrator stumbles from the chapel, shamed beyond words for his betrayal of the college.

He then goes to Dr. Bledsoe, who reprimands him ferociously (**chapter six**). The college president describes the necessity of lying to whites ("[T]he only way to please a white man is to tell him a lie!") and talks about the black man's social invisibility ("You're nobody, son. You don't exist . . ."). He proclaims that he has created a place for himself in the country's all-white society by playing the role of the deferential black yea-sayer. The interview evokes memories of the dying words of the narrator's grandfather who, as Ellison describes in chapter one, led a life of exemplary humility and obedience but declared on his death bed that his acquiescence to whites was actually a subversive ploy to wrest control from them: "I want you to overcome 'em with yeses, undermine 'em with grins . . . let 'em swoller you till they vomit or burst open."

At Dr. Bledsoe's office, the speaker is shocked but relieved to hear that his punishment will be only to leave for the semester. He is sent to New York with Dr. Bledsoe's sealed letters of introduction and told to find work for the summer. On the bus to New York (**chapter seven**), the despondent narrator meets the doctor from the Golden Day again, who also advises him to drop his idealistic notions of race. "Play the game, but don't believe in it . . . ," he tells the hero. Yet the narrator arrives in New York filled with dreams of success. The bustle of the big city temporarily startles him—the intermingling of blacks and whites and the crush of the subway, where he is pushed against an indifferent fat white lady—but he makes his way eagerly to the Men's House in Harlem.

The narrator optimistically reports to various Wall Street offices with Dr. Bledsoe's personal letters but without success. Finally he delivers his last letter to an assistant of a Mr. Emerson (**chapter nine**). In a room draped with exotic tapestries, the dapper white man drops references to Freud and speaks enthusiastically of Harlem nightclubs. After reading the letter, he tries to dissuade the narrator from returning south. Finally he reveals that he is Mr. Emerson's son and shows the narrator Dr. Bledsoe's note, which vows permanent expulsion on the grounds that the narrator, who "has gone grievously astray," is a threat to the school. This betrayal shocks the narrator deeply.

He vows revenge on Dr. Bledsoe and applies for a job at a Long Island paint factory mentioned by Mr. Emerson (**chapter ten**). The narrator is hired because the company does not have to pay union wages to the "colored college boys" it employs. This segment contains some of the most explicit racial symbolism in the novel. Liberty Paints is famed for its "Optic White" paint color, "the purest white that can be found," which it supplies to the government. The paint can only be made by mixing ten drops of a secret formula into buckets of murky black paint. The narrator is set to this task, working frantically but accidentally ruining a batch by using the wrong formula. He is reprimanded and sent to assist Lucius Brockway, the engineer of paint production.

Deep in the basement among the rattling furnaces he meets this wiry old black man, who prefigures his own later underground self. Brockway is both paranoid and belligerent, convinced that the narrator has been sent as a spy. Tenaciously independent, he boasts that he alone knows the secrets of paint making, which the management has tried for years to acquire. He orders the narrator to watch several valve gauges and sets him to work shoveling coal.

During his lunch break, the narrator enters the locker room and discovers a union meeting in session. When the others learn that he works for Brockway, they turn against him, calling him a fink and voting to investigate him. The encounter makes him late for work. When Brockway hears his explanation, he attacks the protagonist in a rage, threatening to kill him, but the narrator eventually overpowers the older man, who breaks down and admits his deep hatred of unions. But at this point one of the valves begins to shriek. Brockway yells to the narrator to turn the white knob and then escapes, laughing, as the valve gives way and the hero is caught in an explosion of white paint. The painful loss of control and consciousness ("Somewhere an engine ground in furious futility, grating loudly until a pain shot around the curve of my head . . .") recalls the end of the boxing match, when the narrator was brutally knocked out.

Chapter eleven recounts one of the most surreal episodes in the novel. The hero wakes up in a white room in the factory hospital. He is strapped to a machine and given electroshock therapy intended (as he overhears a doctor explain) to "produce the results of a prefrontal lobotomy . . . as complete a change of personality as you'll find in your famous fairy-tale cases of criminals transformed into amiable fellows." As his body shakes with the effects of the shocks, he hears one doctor remark, "They really do have rhythm, don't they?"

When the treatment ends, he finds that he can no longer remember his identity. A doctor tells him, "Well, boy, it looks as though you're cured. . . ." The narrator is released, sent to see the director, where he reacts with stabbing pain to the sound of his own name, which begins to trigger his memory. Told to seek work elsewhere, he stumbles back to Harlem, where a maternal woman, Miss Mary, takes pity on him and brings him to her home (**chapter twelve**). He moves into her boarding house and remains there for several peaceful months, unemployed and dependent on Mary's charity but quietly resistant to her lectures on leadership and responsibility.

One cold day he wanders the streets of Harlem and comes across an eviction (**chapter thirteen**). A crowd has gathered near a house where two white men are depositing an old black couple's belongings onto the street. Memories of his childhood return as he stares at the sad household clutter exposed to public scrutiny. When one of the men tries to block the old woman from reentering her home, the crowd threatens to grow violent. The narrator intervenes, calling the people to order with a rousing speech. Yet the man continues to refuse the woman entrance, and the crowd attacks him. The narrator then organizes the crowd to carry the furniture back inside. He controls the carnival atmosphere until the police arrive. Then, running to escape, he is approached by a short red-haired man who calls him "brother" and praises his speech. The man, Brother Jack, invites him to coffee and offers the wary hero a job in his organization. The narrator declines but reconsiders when he remembers his debts to Miss Mary.

In **chapter fourteen** the narrator is introduced to the Brotherhood, a secret quasi-Communist organization whose members meet at swank parties and talk elliptically of their mission to work "for a better world for all people." The narrator is stunned by the posh apartment to which he is taken and moved by Brother Jack's pronouncement of his future as the next Booker T. Washington. The Brotherhood offers him a large salary, provided he sever all ties with his past and adopt a new name and residence. During the ensuing cocktail party, one of the white brothers, thoroughly intoxicated, asks the narrator to sing a black spiritual. Others are embarrassed by his racist stereotyping, and the narrator downplays the offense. Nonetheless he goes home wondering how much he can trust his fellow brothers.

The narrator regretfully leaves Mary's boarding house to the banging of a broken furnace pipe, buying new clothes and moving to an apartment on the Upper East Side (**chapter fifteen**). That evening Brother Jack and a coterie of party members take him to give a speech at a rally in Harlem (**chapter sixteen**). After an initial hesitation, he forges a bond with the audience, rousing them to a fever pitch. The brothers are appalled, deeming the speech politically irresponsible. Because Brother Jack defends him, the narrator is allowed to keep his job on the condition that he go through three months of indoctrination into party principles under the guidance of Brother Hambro. He agrees, leaving the meeting convinced that he has finally found a way "to have a part in making the big decisions, of seeing through the mystery of how the country, the world, really operated."

The novel leaps over the narrator's tutoring to his first assignment as chief spokesman of the Harlem District (**chapter seventeen**). Brother Jack brings him to the district headquarters, where, at the committee meeting, he meets Brother Tod Clifton, a handsome, charismatic young black leader sporting a scar from a recent fight with a rival organization of black nationalists. The hero also meets the head of this organization, the radical black separatist Ras the Exhorter, when he and Clifton organize a street rally. Ras's henchmen break up the gathering, knocking out street lamps and beating men with lead pipes. The scene, pitting blacks against blacks, recalls the earlier battle royal. At one point Ras knocks Clifton down and threatens him with a knife, demanding his reason for staying with the interracial Brotherhood: "You my brother, mahn. Brothers are the same color. . . ." In an impassioned speech Ras emphasizes the need for black solidarity and repeatedly tries to convince Clifton, whom he calls a "black king," to join his party. The narrator breaks up the fight and ignores Ras's threats, but Clifton admits that he is troubled by the speech and wonders if "sometimes a man has to plunge outside history."

Nonetheless the narrator proves a successful organizer, and within weeks the Brotherhood clinches power in the district.

The narrator's fame spreads rapidly: for a short stretch he lives "dominated by the all-embracing idea of Brotherhood." Then he receives an anonymous letter warning him of jealousy among the white leaders (**chapter eighteen**). Soon a white member, Brother Wrestrum, accuses the narrator of self-promotion. In a scene evoking the arbitrary vindictiveness of the union meeting, the members vote for an investigation and order the narrator temporarily demoted, sending him downtown to lecture on the "Woman Question."

In **chapter nineteen** the narrator gives his first speech on women's issues, and an eager female member of the audience invites him home to discuss the question further. In her elegant apartment, she aggressively seduces him. Afterward, he worries that the affair might have been a setup to orchestrate his downfall. But a more urgent problem intervenes. Brother Clifton disappears, and the narrator is asked to return to the rudderless Harlem District.

He finds that during his month-long absence the Brotherhood has fallen into disrepute in Harlem (**chapter twenty**). Patrons confront him at the local bar, the district headquarters are deserted, and he is pointedly excluded from the central committee's meeting. Walking along Forty-third Street after enduring this latest affront, he stops to listen to a street vendor's spiel and recognizes Clifton selling "Sambo Boogie Woogie paper dolls." Before the narrator can confront him, Clifton disappears to avoid the police. The hero, amazed, wanders on and runs into the sideshow a second time. When a policeman barks at Clifton, his patience breaks, and he turns and knocks the officer down. As Clifton crouches to spring, the cop shoots him dead. After witnessing this horrific tableau, the narrator roams the streets bewildered by Clifton's desertion. He watches a group of apolitical zoot-suiters riding the subway back to Harlem and witnesses a petty shoplifting, wondering what real effect the Brotherhood has had on the black community.

Returning to his office, the narrator throws his energy into an open-air funeral for Clifton. The public showing is tremendous, yet when he stands to give the funeral address the narrator finds his political ideology falls flat. He makes a despondent, fatalistic pronouncement. He returns to his office to discover it full of grim-faced white party members, who call Clifton a traitor and accuse the narrator of playing up the race issue (**chapter twenty-two**). When the narrator insists that he was giving the people of Harlem the guidance and action they craved, Brother Jack answers, "We do not shape our policies to the mistaken and infantile notions of the man on the street. Our job is not to ask them what they think, but to *tell* them!" Brother Jack shocks the narrator by pulling out his own eye—it is artificial!—and dropping it in a glass of water. His real eye had been lost in the name of discipline, he says, admonishing the hero to obey with the same selflessness.

The brothers leave the protagonist to wander the darkened streets of Harlem, where he runs across Ras leading a rally (**chapter twenty-three**). The two argue about Clifton's death, and the narrator leaves to escape Ras's henchmen. He decides to disguise himself, but when he buys a pair of dark sunglasses and a wide-brimmed hat, he is immediately mistaken for someone named Rinehart. A heavily perfumed young woman tries to pick him up. Above the summer blare of cars and radios, he hears Ras continuing to incite the crowd. The black leader yells, "It is time Ras the Exhorter become Ras the DESTROYER!" and calls for action. In this mood of increasing tension, passersby continue to mistake the hero for Rinehart. He learns through his various encounters that the man is a womanizer, gambler, mob leader, and pimp. Then he stumbles into a church meeting and realizes that Rinehart is also a crooked minister, robbing his elderly congregation of their cash.

The narrator makes a last-ditch effort to restore his beliefs, visiting his former party tutor, Hambro, who tells him that the party's control of the Harlem District will have to be sacrificed for the greater good of the Brotherhood. Here he learns that "Rinehartism—cynicism" is not far from party policy: Hambro dismisses his charges of charlatanism with the argument that "it's impossible not to take advantage of the people." The narrator sees in the party's call for "scientific objectivity" the cruelty of the factory hospital's shock-therapy machine. He leaves angry and disillusioned, determined to imitate Rinehart and follow his grandfather's advice to gain control of the organization: "They were forcing me to Rinehart's methods, so bring on the scientists?"

He begins by downplaying his district's incidents of violence and falsifying a new list of members. The tactic seems to work, and he regains favor at the next meeting. He also hatches a plan to seduce an important member's wife to learn secret information. He finds a willing partner in a rich, lonely white woman named Sybil, married to one of the Brotherhood's "big shots," whom he invites to his apartment. Here he plies her with drinks and presses her for secrets. Unfortunately she has nothing to tell but, in an increasingly drunken fervor, urges him to enact a rape scene with her. The hero, both disgusted and amused, watches her drop off to sleep. They are roused by a phone call reporting riots in Harlem. Drunkenly stumbling into the night, the narrator tries to procure Sybil a taxi, while she begs to be taken along. He sends her downtown, but she reappears, running barefoot along 110th Street. He finds another cab, finally cajoling her to leave.

The narrator arrives in Harlem to find a nightmarish cityscape of shattered storefronts and surging bands of looters (**chapter twenty-five**). Alarms wail and gunshots ring out. He falls, nicked in the head by a bullet, but some men help him up, and he joins their band of looters, passing through streets of carnivalesque abandon. Their leader, Dupre, organizes the burning of a run-down tenement that his landlord has refused to fix. Amid various protests, he and his men torch the disease-ridden building.

The narrator runs on in the dark, stopping to help a man twist his own tourniquet and dodging police. He realizes that the Brotherhood must have planned the race riot, sacrificing Harlem for the sake of propaganda. His cynical acquiescence has not served as resistance to the Brotherhood, but rather as a tool, facilitating the party's plan. A final chilling image arrests his thoughts—seven naked white female mannequins hanging from a lamppost.

Then, as in a nightmare, he sees Ras the Destroyer dressed in the costume of an Abyssinian chieftain charging at him on horseback. The narrator protests that Ras, too, is being manipulated by the Brotherhood: "They deserted you so that in your despair you'd follow this man to your destruction." Ras throws a spear at the narrator, calling him a traitor and ordering him to be hanged. As he faces imminent death, the narrator realizes the absurdity of the causes he has supported and the hatred soon to bring about his death, as well as the truth about his own invisibility—he is just one small black man about to be extinguished by another. Empowered by the thought that it is "better to live out one's own absurdity than die for that of others," he throws Ras's spear, catching the chieftain in the jaw, and narrowly escapes through a looted store.

He tries to make his way downtown, stumbling with the blind disorientation experienced in so many of the novel's climaxes. A gang of hoodlums see him and give chase. While running, he falls through an open manhole into a coal cellar. When he refuses to give the gang his briefcase, they cover the hole, trapping him. He tries to burn a torch by lighting all of the important documents he has saved—his high school diploma, his Brotherhood papers, the paper doll from Brother Clifton—but cannot find a way out. Caught in a "state neither of dreaming nor of waking," he has a vision of disputing his former role models and disavowing his earlier illusions. He awakes to the realization that he cannot return to his former life.

Ellison's narration now returns to the fictional present, with a tentatively optimistic **epilogue**. Having made the cellar his home and having realized that the world outside is just as "concrete, ornery, vile and sublimely wonderful as before," the narrator finally tells us "that America is woven of many strands; I would recognize them and let it so remain. . . . Life is to be lived, not controlled; and humanity is won by continuing to play in the face of certain defeat." Despite the fact that he cannot be seen, he concludes that "there's a possibility that even an invisible man has a socially responsible role to play." In a decision that suggests Ellison's lingering hope for public action in race relations, the narrator ends by announcing his plan to break his hibernation.

Critical Views

Cultural Context of *Invisible Man*: *Brown v. Board of Education*

In dealing with the question of the effects of segregation, it must be recognized that these effects do not take place in a vacuum, but in a social context. The segregation of Negroes and of other groups in the United States takes place in a social milieu in which "race" prejudice and discrimination exist. It is questionable in the view of some students of the problem whether it is possible to have segregation without substantial discrimination. . . . The imbeddedness of segregation in such a context makes it difficult to disentangle the effects of segregation *per se* from the effects of the context. Similarly, it is difficult to disentangle the effects of segregation from the effects of a pattern of social disorganization commonly associated with it and reflected in high disease and mortality rates, crime and delinquency, poor housing, disrupted family life and general substandard living conditions.

At the recent Mid-century White House Conference on Children and Youth, a fact-finding report on the effects of prejudice, discrimination, and segregation on the personality development of children was prepared as a basis for some of the deliberations. . . . It highlighted the fact that segregation, prejudices and discriminations, and their social concomitants potentially damage the personality of all children—the children of the majority group in a somewhat different way than the more obviously damaged children of the minority group.

The report indicates that as minority group children learn the inferior status to which they are assigned—as they observe the fact that they are almost always segregated and kept apart from others who are treated with more respect by the society as a whole—they often react with feelings of inferiority and a sense of personal humiliation. Many of them become confused about their own personal worth. On the one hand, like all other human beings they require a sense of personal dignity; on the other hand, almost nowhere in the larger society do they find their own dignity as human beings respected by others. Under these conditions, the minority group child is thrown into a conflict with regard to his feelings about himself and his group. He wonders whether his group and he himself are worthy of no more respect than they receive. This conflict and confusion leads to self-hatred and rejection of his own group.

The report goes on to point out that these children must find ways with which to cope with this conflict. . . .

Some children, usually of the lower socioeconomic classes, may react by overt aggressions and hostility directed toward their own group or members of the dominant group. Anti-social and delinquent behavior may often be interpreted as reactions to these racial frustrations. These reactions are self-destructive in that the larger society not only punishes those who commit them, but often interprets such aggressive and anti-social behavior as justification for continuing prejudice and segregation.

Middle class and upper class minority group children are likely to react to their racial frustrations and conflicts by withdrawal and submissive behavior. Or, they may react with compensatory and rigid conformity to the prevailing middle class values and standards and an aggressive determination to succeed in these terms in spite of the handicap of their minority status.

The report indicates that minority group children of all social and economic classes often react with a generally defeatist attitude and a lowering of personal ambitions. This, for example, is reflected in a lowering of pupil morale and a depression of the educational aspiration level among minority group children in segregated schools. In producing such effects, segregated schools impair the ability of the child to profit from the educational opportunities provided him.

Many minority group children of all classes also tend to be hypersensitive and anxious about their relations with the larger society. They tend to see hostility and rejection even in those areas where these might not actually exist.

The report concludes that while the range of individual differences among members of a rejected minority group is as wide as among other peoples, the evidence suggests that all of these children are unnecessarily encumbered in some ways by segregation and its concomitants. . . .

Conclusions similar to those reached by the Mid-century White House Conference Report have been stated by other social scientists who have concerned themselves with this problem. The following are some examples of these conclusions:

Segregation imposes upon individuals a distorted sense of social reality.

Segregation leads to a blockage in the communications and interaction between the two groups. Such blockages tend to increase mutual suspicion, distrust and hostility.

Segregation not only perpetuates rigid stereotypes and reinforces negative attitudes toward members of the other group, but also leads to the development of a social climate within which violent outbreaks of racial tensions are likely to occur. . . .

On the basis of this general fund of knowledge, it seems likely that feelings of inferiority and doubts about personal worth are attributable to living in an underprivileged environment only insofar as the latter is itself perceived as an indicator of low social status and as a symbol of inferiority. In other words, one of the important determinants in producing such feelings is the awareness of social status difference. While there are many other factors that serve as reminders of the differences in social status, there can be little doubt that the fact of enforced segregation is a major factor.

RALPH ELLISON ON PROTEST IN *INVISIBLE MAN*

Sir, was it your intention to include any protest in the novel?

Protest in the novel?

Yes sir, would you call it a protest novel?

I would think that implicitly the novel protests. It protests the agonies of growing up. It protests the problem of trying to find a way into a complex, intricately structured society in a way which would allow this particular man to behave in a manly way and which would allow him to seize some instrumentalities of political power. That is where the protest is on one level. On another level, the protest lies in my trying to make a story out of these elements without falling into the clichés which have marked and marred most fiction about American Negroes, that is, to write literature instead of political protest. Beyond this, I would say very simply that in the very act of trying to create something there is implicit a protest against the way things are—a protest against man's vulnerability before the larger forces of society and the universe. We make fiction out of that kind of protest which is similar to the kind of protest that is involved in your mastering your bodies; your mastering the disciplines—the physical and intellectual disciplines, the military disciplines, the legal disciplines—which you are here for. All of this is a protest, a human protest against that which is, against the raw and unformed way that we come into the world. I don't think you have to demand any more protest than that of the novelist. I think, on the other hand, if he tells the truth, if he writes eloquently and depicts believable human beings and believable human situations, then he has done more than simply protest. I think that his task is to present the human, to make it eloquent, and to provide some sense of transcendence over the given, that is, to make his protest meaningful, significant, and eloquent of human value.

Larry Neal on Ellison's Place in the Art versus Politics Conflict

There is quite a bit of discussion about the nature of history in Ellison's *Invisible Man*. Along with the obvious theme of identity, the nameless narrator is constantly in search of a "useable past." In order to arrive at an understanding of the complex dimensions of his American experience, Ellison plunged deep into the murky world of mythology and folklore, both of which are essential elements in the making of a people's history. But Ellison's history is non-dialectical. The novel attempts to construct its own universe, based on its own imperatives, the central ones being the shaping of a personal vision, as in the blues, and the celebration of a collective vision as is represented by the living culture. And it is the living culture, with all of its shifting complexities, which constitutes the essential landscape of the novel. The unnamed narrator questions the "scientific" history of the "Brotherhood" and in one of the most intense sections of the novel asks the following question: ". . . What if Brother Jack were wrong? What if history was a gambler, instead of a force in a laboratory experiment, and the boys his ace in the hole? What if history was not a reasonable citizen, but a madman full of paranoid guile . . . ?"

This discourse follows the death of Tod Clifton, a man who had previously been described as having fallen "outside of history." Tottering between contending political forces, i.e., the rigid dogmas of the "Brotherhood," and the emotionally compelling rhetoric of Ras, the Exhorter, Tod attempts to leap outside of historical time altogether. And he ultimately leaps to his death.

Churning way beneath the surface of the novel's narrative is a fantastically rich and engaging mythic and folkloristic universe. Further, this universe is introduced to us through the music of Louis Armstrong. Louis' music, then, forms the overall structure for the novel. If that is the case, the subsequent narrative and all of the action which follows can be read as one long blues solo. . . .

Invisible Man [has] a very unique aesthetic. There has been much talk of late about a "black aesthetic," but there has been, fundamentally, a failure to examine those elements of the Black experience in America which could genuinely constitute an aesthetic. With no real knowledge of folk culture—blues, folk songs, folk narratives, spirituals, dance styles, gospels, speech, and oral history—there is very little possibility that a black aesthetic will be realized in our literature.

Ellison, on the other hand, finds the aesthetic all around him. He finds it in memories of his Oklahoma background. He finds it in preachers, blues singers, hustlers, gamblers, jazz men, boxers, dancers, and itinerant storytellers. He notes carefully the subtleties of American speech patterns. He pulls the covers off the stereotypes in order to probe beneath the surface where the hard-core mythic truth lies. He keeps checking out style. The way people walk, what they say and what they leave unsaid. If anyone has been concerned with a "black aesthetic" it has certainly got to be Ralph Ellison. And even if you disagree with Ellison's political thrust these days, you have got to dig his consistent concern for capturing the essential truths of the Black man's experience in America.

And where are these essential truths embodied, if not in the folk culture? Do not Stagalee, High John The Conqueror, John Henry, Shine, and the Signifying Monkey reveal vital aspects of our group experience? Or has the current "rediscovery" of African culture obscured the fact that however disruptive slavery must have been to our original African personalities, our fathers and mothers intuitively understood what aspect of it could be rescued and reshaped. And did not this reshaping indicate a *willed* desire to survive and maintain one's own specific outlook on life. Didn't it exhibit a willed desire to survive in the face of danger? What kind of people were they in their weaknesses and their strengths? Haven't we read their slave narratives, and listened carefully to their songs? And hasn't the essential spirit that they breathed into these expressions continued to manifest itself in all meaningful aspects of our struggle? We must address ourselves to this kind of humanity because it is meaningful and within our immediate reach. To do so means understanding something essential about the persistency of tradition, and also understanding the manner in which values are shaped out of tradition. And what's more important, values whose fundamental function was to bind us together into a community of shared feelings and memories in order that we might survive. . . .

All Black creative artists owe Ellison special gratitude. He and a few others of his generation have struggled to keep the culture alive in their artistic works. We should not be content with merely basking in the glow of their works. We need what they have given us. But the world has changed. Which is as it should. And we have changed in the world. Which is quite natural. Because everybody and everything is change. However, what Ellison teaches us is that it is not possible to move toward meaningful creative ends without somehow taking with you the accumulated weight of your forebears' experiences. . . .

The poet, the writer, is a key bearer of culture. Through myth, he is the manipulator of both the collective conscious and unconscious. If he is good, he is the master of rhetorical imagery. And as such, he is much more psychically powerful than the secular politician. And that is why he is, to some extent, in some societies, feared and suppressed by secular politicians. Sometimes, he is suppressed even by the laity who must finally embrace his art, if it is to live. But the suppression of art, whether it occurs in the West or in the East, whether it occurs under capitalism or socialism, is detrimental to Man's spiritual survival. Without spirit, the substance of all of his material accomplishments means essentially nothing. Therefore, what we might consider is a system of politics and art that is as fluid, as functional, and as expansive as Black music. No such system now exists, we're gonna have to build it. And when it is finally realized, it will be a conglomerate, gleaned from the whole of all of our experiences.

Kerry McSweeney on Influences on *Invisible Man*

The forms of black American artistic expression that most influenced *Invisible Man* were folklore, jazz, and the blues. . . . For Ellison, folklore offered "the first drawings of any group's character" and was the record of its attempts "to humanize the world."

> It preserves mainly those situations which have repeated themselves again and again in the history of any given group. It describes those rites, manners, customs, and so forth, which insure the good life, or destroy it; and

> it describes those boundaries of feeling, thought and action which that particular group has found to be the limitation of the human condition. It projects this wisdom in symbols which express the group's will to survive; it embodies those values by which the group lives and dies.

Folklore, then, was essential to the understanding and to the depiction of the informing spirit of black America. Moreover, a novelist who could learn to employ these motifs in his work could add richness to its texture and attain a degree of formal organization that increased the work's resonance. . . .

Jazz was a different kind of formal influence on *Invisible Man*. Ellison's sense of this mode of creative expression was rooted in the example of the jazzmen he had known during his youth. Their "driving motivation" had been "the will to achieve the most eloquent expression of idea-emotions through mastery of their instruments. . . . The end of all this discipline and technical mastery was the desire to express an affirmative way of life through [a] musical tradition . . . that insisted that each artist achieve his creativity within its frame. He must learn the best of the past, and add to it his personal vision." The influence of the blues was more direct and more pervasive. Not only are there blues singers within *Invisible Man* (including Jim Trueblood, Mary Rambo, and the cartman in chapter 9 who calls himself Peter Wheatstraw); the whole novel, which begins with its narrator listening to a blues song of Louis Armstrong, can be seen as "a blues odyssey" or rather as "the literary extension of the blues. It was as if Ellison had taken an everyday twelve-bar blues tune (by a man from down South sitting [underground] up North in New York singing and signifying about how he got there) and scored it for full orchestra." As Ellison explained in an essay written the same year he began *Invisible Man*: "The blues is an impulse to keep the painful details and episodes of a brutal experience alive in one's aching consciousness, to finger its jagged grain, and to transcend it, not by the consolation of philosophy but by squeezing from it a near-tragic, near-comic lyricism. As a form, the blues is an autobiographical chronicle of personal catastrophe expressed lyrically."

Important as folklore motifs, the jazzmen's example, and blues rhythms are to *Invisible Man*, these distinctive forms of black-American creative expression are not the predominant artistic influences on the novel. The informing artistic context is more literary and more richly varied. As Ellison has explained, what is "most important of all" in writing a novel, even more than "what you seek to depict," is perspective. "And the main perspective through which a writer looks at experience is that provided by literature—just as the perspective through which a physician looks at the human body is the discipline of medicine; an accumulation of techniques, insights, instruments, and processes which have been slowly developed over long periods of time." One lens through which Ellison looked at his subject was Dostoyevski's great novella *Notes from Underground* (1864), whose anonymous first-person narrator sits alone in his room brooding and thinking, tells the story of how he got to be where he is, and ends, like Ellison's protagonist, by suggesting that at some deep level he speaks for the reader. But more important than these resemblances, as Joseph Frank has observed, was "Ellison's profound grasp of the ideological inspiration of Dostoyevski's work, and his perception of its relevance to his own creative purposes—his perception, that is, of how he could use Dostoyevski's relation to the Russian culture of his time to express his own position as an American Negro writer in relation to the dominating white culture."

T. S. Eliot and James Joyce are other ancestors. While at Tuskegee, Ellison had discovered Eliot's *Waste Land*, and had been impressed by its range of allusion and by the closeness to the jazz experience of the sensibility he found in the poem. . . . Like Eliot, Joyce helped to make Ellison aware of the playful possibilities of language, and no one who has read them both will doubt that the mixture of realistic and symbolic levels in *Ulysses*, as well as its stylistic and presentational variations, were a considerable influence on *Invisible Man*. André Malraux was another ancestor; his novels expressed a concern "with the individual caught up consciously in an historical situation" and provided nondeterministic insights "which allowed me to understand certain possibilities in the fictional material around me." So was Hemingway; Ellison's strictures on Hemingway's limitations of vision and absorption in technique have to be supplemented by his acknowledgment of the elder writer's importance as "in many ways the true father-as-artist of so many of us who came to writing during the late thirties." . . .

[To] the importance of the principal nineteenth-century American novelists and their moral commitment to Ellison's conception of the novelist's task . . . should be added a word about the tradition of American humor, particularly the line that runs from southwestern humor through Mark Twain and on to William Faulkner and Erskine Caldwell, whose *Tobacco Road* made Ellison aware of the liberating potential of extravagant laughter. Such a perspective perhaps deserves more emphasis than it is often given by commentators, for *Invisible Man* not only makes use of comic motifs, it is also frequently a very funny book. Finally, there is the influence and example of William Faulkner, the greatest American novelist of the twentieth century, an influence by no means restricted to the all-hell-breaks-loose humor in *Invisible Man*. The most important point is that in his work Faulkner continued the moral tradition that was at the heart of the work of the nineteenth-century American novelists, and was himself an example of what the creative activity of the novelist could achieve. "He was born," Ellison has said, "with all the anti-Negro clichés of Deep South white society, but as he confronted his own work, he discovered the human reality that lay behind these stereotypes. In the end, he wrote more deeply about Negroes than most Negro writers. I'd like to achieve the same kind of freedom as a Negro writer and as a man."

Alan Nadel on Invisible Man and Huck and Jim

Ellison's most important allusions to *Huckleberry Finn* . . . come in chapter 10, the Liberty Paints factory episode. The chapter begins: "The plant was in Long Island, and I crossed a bridge in the fog to get there and came down in a stream of workers. Ahead of me a huge electric sign announced its message through the drifting strands of fog: KEEP AMERICA PURE WITH LIBERTY PAINTS" (149). A few paragraphs later, the invisible man's name is entered on the "shipping department's payroll." The words "island," "bridge," "stream," "drifting," and "shipping," together with the three appearances in the first paragraph of the word "fog"—not a common image in *Invisible Man*—suggest a stream or a river in the fog. Passing through this fog, the invisible man finds himself mixing black dope into the white paint, made white by the unseen presence of that dope. "Slowly," he says, "I measured the glistening black drops, seeing them settle upon the surface and become blacker still, spreading suddenly out to the edges" (152). Though diminished and reversed, this replicates the famous image of the white Ohio River trailing along the edge of the muddy Mississippi before disappearing into it.

In *Huckleberry Finn* that image appears as a sign that Huck and Jim have passed the point of turning back, of going up the Ohio into the free states. It tells them they must have passed Cairo in the fog. The events in the paint factory, similarly, end the invisible man's hopes of reversing the direction of his journey. He had entered the factory as a way of earning money to return to the college to kill Bledsoe. The image of the white paint absorbing the black dope, however, hints that the invisible man, too, will be absorbed in the white world to which he has come rather than return for any reason to the black college. It also foreshadows his story in a more literal way. At the end of the paint factory episode, having fallen for Brockway's trick, he will be absorbed in the exploding white paint. Then he will be given an electric lobotomy and left, with small compensation, to be lost in the dark periphery of New York. As the white Ohio does in *Huckleberry Finn*, the black dope in *Invisible Man* provides a visual image which both tells the reader that a character has passed the point of turning back and signifies his plight.

By reversing the imagery, Ellison shows us once again that an allusion is always both same and different. The differences in this case can remind us that the direction of the journeys are opposite, that in a manner of speaking the invisible man is fulfilling Jim's wish to go north. Considering *Huckleberry Finn* in these terms raises the possibility that the promise of the Ohio was no more likely to meet Jim's expectations than his hopeless drifting to the South. The clear water of the Ohio may have represented the purity of freedom, as the mud of the Mississippi may have the impurity of slavery, but the white in the factory is paint, an impure substance made under the misleading sign of purity, a bogus purity which covers up, whitewashes, makes the black dope invisible.

In many ways, Jim, too, is an invisible man, not the fully realized character that Huck is. As Ellison, among others, has noted, *Huckleberry Finn* is not Jim's story. Huck and Jim have different goals on the raft, and while Huck wants in some ways to remain on the raft forever, Jim wants to get off it and to be free. The moral burden of Jim's quest makes Huck abandon his own, and Jim's primary importance is in what he represents for Huck. Despite his great symbolic importance, however, Ellison, as we have seen, finds Jim as a character in his own right greatly lacking.

By associating Jim with the invisible man, therefore, Ellison points out the ways in which Jim is invisible. At the same time, however, Ellison's imagery highlights the dilemma of which both he and Twain were well aware—that there was no place for Jim to go. In seeing, as the paint-bucket reversal suggests, that the journey north is only another way of going downriver, we see in yet another version the true impossibility of Jim's situation, and we see that the problem of *Huckleberry Finn* is not that Twain is caught in the flow of a river heading only toward enslavement. Rather, especially writing from the perspective of the failure of Reconstruction, Twain understood the problem was not regional but an illness of the shore, of being "sivilized." The Brothers up north, as Ellison will show us, are just latter-day Tom Sawyers. . . .

The diminishing in size from river to bucket also serves to underscore Jim's symbolic status. The invisible man must lose ten drops of black dope in each of many white buckets, all heading for the national monument. The one drop of black dope is one of many, each invisible, all serving myriad goals, in many proper places making the white surface look whiter. In this way, Ellison comments on those who would discount Huck's lesson on the raft. Certainly Huck has not turned into an abolitionist, has not abandoned his ideas about race and slavery. Yet both Twain and Ellison understood the symbolic importance of Huck's commitment to Jim in that both authors knew that any commitment is meaningless in the form of dogma. The power of Huck's commitment comes from its arising out of an understanding between human beings, which contrasts sharply with Tom's inhumane commitments. As Tom is capable only of seeing through books, Huck is incapable of doing so. Thus he cannot learn the lesson of Moses and the Bullrushes from a book, but learns it in practice, being cast out upon the water for salvation, taken for dead, reborn, and eventually taking the slave from Cairo to freedom.

The end of chapter 10 also closely parallels a scene in *Huckleberry Finn*, the sinking of the raft. Very shortly after discovering the traces of the Ohio in the Mississippi, Huck and Jim formulate a new plan—to buy passage up the river—but that, too, is ruined when a riverboat sinks their raft; this first puts them in a state of limbo, then abruptly changes their plans. The explosion in the boiler room has a similar effect on the invisible man at exactly the same point in his story. In many ways, moreover, the details and imagery in the two scenes are very similar.

Walter Slatoff on Staying Human and Sane in *Invisible Man*

"You won't believe in my invisibility and you'll fail to see how any principle that applies to you could apply to me. You'll fail to see it even though death waits for both of us if you don't" (567). . . ."Who knows but that on the lower frequencies I speak for you." . . . Whitman's "Song of Myself" begins with the word *I* and ends with the word *you*. . . .

More important than the direct speaking tone and I–you dialectic . . . is that the telling is itself a way of surviving for the hero of the book, a way of handling his anger and bitterness, of staying somewhat human, of forcing himself to love as well as to hate. . . . "So why do I write torturing myself . . ." (566). . . . In addition to the cathartic and possibly redemptive aspects of the telling [is] the confusion and pain it entails and the ironies involved in the effort since the narrator knows that one of the tricks of those who controlled him was to keep him hoping. . . . The word *torturing* is no mere literary exaggeration and . . . what most governs the tone of the book is a kind of torment—the kind that comes from looking at yourself as unsparingly and honestly as you can, from recognizing that you haven't solved the crucial problems you are examining, from knowing that you are still terribly enmeshed with what you have undergone, and from refusing to accept phony answers or resolutions. What we are witnessing ultimately in this book (and in certain other black writers like James Baldwin) is the effort of a person to cope fully with the mental and emotional damage caused by having grown up black in a white society—the effort of such a person, that is, to stay sane.

This is no mere liberal platitude. . . . How does one go through what the young man has experienced in this book without going crazy? You can, in the terms of the book, remain frozen, keep your eye on the white line, keep running; but once you seriously let yourself be human, real chaos threatens. . . . The young man summarizes his experience in terms of freezing and thawing and speaks of the ice as melting into a flood in which he threatens to drown (253–54). . . . Ellison and Baldwin have allowed themselves to thaw and let the flood come and then faced the nearly impossible task of staying mentally (and sometimes rhetorically) afloat. . . . [The] damage done to many black people goes far beyond the infliction of poverty and the other usual injuries sometimes recognized by the white world. What they face, and what this book is mostly about . . . is the struggle to become human and stay sane. . . . [Look at] the insanity and real chaos of the veterans of the Golden Day saloon, the implications of the "Supercargo" and superego that "censor" and control them, and the final hysteria (laughter and tears) of the "crazy" brain surgeon. . . . [W]hen the young man isn't frozen, nearly every aspect of his experience seems to call for both laughter and tears . . . laughter is often what does enable him to cope.

How do you stay sane . . . after going through even the single experience of the smoker described in the opening chapter; an experience involving fighting your own kind, blindness, sex, drunkenness, scrabbling for money, electric shocks, humiliation and reward, simultaneous hatred of whites and other blacks and of yourself, the acceptance of a briefcase, containing a scholarship given to you by men you have to hate and fear and who you know have contempt for you for taking it, and unbearably conflicting feelings toward a nude white dancer. . . .

How do you stay sane . . . when in addition to the problems of identity everyone faces growing up, you must face the further problems that you have no name or that your name is that of your former slave masters; that you have been taught to despise the traditions and ways of being that have been part of the little identity you do have; that even when you have learned not to despise those traditions, you can't find an identity that seems helpful or relevant in the world as you see it about you. . . . [The] young man does learn not to be ashamed of Mary Rambo and . . . he comes to see her as "a force, a stable, familiar force" like something from his past that prevented him "from whirling off into some unknown which [he] dared not face" (252). And he gains a wonderful sense of freedom when he unashamedly eats yams on the street, a sense of freedom associated with the ability to laugh and perhaps with the power he is able to exert at the eviction of the old black couple. But his new awareness doesn't help enough, as we learn from the passage in which he sadly thinks how, now that he no longer feels ashamed of the things he has always loved, he probably can "no longer digest very many of them." Realizing that he can't live simply at the yam level, he finds the end of the yam unpleasant, "frost-bitten" (260–61). . . .

The book does not . . . give . . . much hope; . . . certain kinds of human damage can't be repaired, . . . all the king's horses and all the king's men can't put Humpty-Dumpty together again. . . . [T]he damage is as irreparable as it is because the young man was never encouraged or even allowed to discover what he wanted and that this meant he had no self to fall back on even when he saw through what was being done to him. . . .

The damage is irreparable . . . because he can't find a way either to ignore his grandfather and all the other Sambo figures or to accept them fully. He keeps trying to throw away the Sambo coin bank he finds in Mary Rambo's house but can't get rid of it. He wants both to laugh at the Sambo dolls Clifton is selling and to destroy them. . . . The invisible man's ultimate dilemma is that the doll is a part of his heritage but one he can neither deny nor accept. To deny it is one kind of nonhumanity; to accept it is another kind of dehumanization. And the choices are fraught with danger. The white crowd loves Sambo, but when the white cop calls Clifton "nigger" and he turns on the cop like a man and not a Sambo, the cop shoots him. . . .

[The] essence of that irreparable injury [is that the] white world of the past gave the black man no alternatives between being Sambo and being dead, and at the same time it despised him for being Sambo. Then it said to Sambo's children and grandchildren and great grandchildren: If you can learn to be like us and despise Sambo, too, we'll let you share in some of our goodies. And then the white world wonders why so many black people won't buy it. . . .

[A] ray of hope . . . is that despite his having decided that the whole struggle is essentially absurd and that he is invisible, the narrator continues to recognize that invisibility is a kind of sickness and that to remain human he has to love as well as hate. And he wants to feel human. At the end of the book, although it means more pain and conflict than remaining underground, he is planning to come out of his hole, to try again. Even though he is quite sure it is no use, that "[y]ou won't believe in my invisibility and you'll fail to see it even though death waits for both of us if you don't" (567), he will to become visible. . . .

[Think] about . . . the incredible extent to which people do not look at one another, do not do so in most communities. . . .

[We] act as though we do not see one another and are not seen, act in such a way as to make ourselves and others invisible. . . . Is that perhaps what the invisible man is finally most afraid of—that terrible tendency in all of us to inflict invisibility on others and in some sense to choose it? Why do we do this? What is it we're so afraid of? The discomfort of being and feeling human?

Eric J. Sundquist on Ralph Ellison, Jazz, and Louis Armstrong

Ellison's own training as a musician, as well as his several unsurpassed essays on jazz and the blues, has frequently provided readers a key to the stylistic virtuosity and improvisatory development of character and idea in *Invisible Man*. . . . Some of the greatest jazz musicians have gone unrecorded or have witnessed their most original ideas pass immediately, and often anonymously, into the public domain. . . . The endless improvisation on traditional materials, as well as the invention of new melodic techniques, defines both the resilience of his hero in *Invisible Man* and Ellison's own attitude toward his novelistic craft.

It is therefore no mistake that Louis Armstrong is invoked in the Prologue of *Invisible Man* for his ability to make "poetry out of being invisible." Listening to Armstrong's rendition of "What Did I Do to Be So Black and Blue" while high on marijuana, the protagonist discovers that invisibility "gives one a slightly different sense of time, you're never quite on the beat. Sometimes you're ahead and sometimes you're behind. Instead of the swift and imperceptible flowing of time, you are aware of its nodes, those points where time stands still or from which it leaps ahead. And you slip into the breaks and look around" (*Invisible Man* 8). Among the many respects in which his novel might be compared to a jazz composition or performance, Ellison's sense of history as a form of subjective temporality—a constructed story, not a set of objective facts—is perhaps the most profound. His intricate individual variations, or riffs, on motifs or images, as well as the protagonist's self-evident improvisation of new identities in a spiraling serial of new circumstances, are lesser elements of the book's grander design, which narrates the course of modern African American life in the nameless protagonist's experiences. . . .

To the extent that his inclusive vision of the writer's sources and obligations crossed racial lines and sprang from his sense that the grave flaws in America's democratic dream could be redeemed, Ellison, one might say, found himself in something of the same predicament he appreciated in Louis Armstrong. Armstrong's willingness to use his vocal and instrumental art to reach a broad American audience provoked accusations among the purists of a younger bebop generation of the 1940s and 1950s that he, arguably the greatest innovator in jazz history, had become a comic Uncle Tom (Ellison, "The Golden Age, Time Past" 211). The Louis Armstrong to whom one might best compare Ellison, though, was the one he himself elsewhere identified as a trickster, a figure capable of adapting to adverse circumstances through inventive disguises and forceful displays of wit. Like Armstrong, this Ralph Ellison is a figure whose putting on of a deceptive mask is "motivated not so much by fear as by a profound rejection of the image created to usurp his identity," a figure whose "clownish license and intoxicating powers" are a sign of kinship with other American tricksters such as Benjamin Franklin, whom Ellison frequently cited as an adroit manipulator of the paradoxes of democracy (Ellison, "Change the Joke and Slip the Yoke" 52–55). And it is the Ralph Ellison who found in Armstrong's music a suitable analogy for the complexities of T. S. Eliot's masterpiece of modernist poetry, *The Waste Land*, which Ellison first studied as a student at Tuskegee Institute and later often cited as an influence on *Invisible Man*: "Somehow [the poem's] rhythms were often closer to those of jazz than were those of the Negro poets, and . . . its range of allusion was as mixed and as varied as that of Louis Armstrong" (Ellison, "Hidden Name and Complex Fate" 154–60). . . .

Out in the street, shufflin' feet,
Couples passing two by two,

While here am I, left high and dry,
Black, and 'cause I'm black I'm blue.

Browns and yellers all have fellers,
Gentlemen prefer them light,
Wish I could fade, can't make the grade,
Nothin' but dark days in sight.

Cold empty bed, springs hard as lead,
Pains in my head, feel like old Ned,
What did I do to be so black and blue?

No joys for me, no company,
Even the mouse ran from my house,
All my life through, I've been so black and blue,

I'm white inside, it don't help my case,
'Cause I can't hide what is on my face.

I'm so forlorn, life's just a thorn,
My heart is torn, why was I born?
What did I do to be so black and blue?

Just 'cause you're black, folks think you lack,
They laugh at you and scorn you too,
What did I do to be so black and blue?

When you are near, they laugh and sneer,
Set you aside and you're denied,
What did I do to be so black and blue?

How sad I am, each day I feel worse,
My mark of Ham seems to be a curse.

How will it end? Ain't got a friend,
My only sin is in my skin,
What did I do to be so black and blue?

JOHN F. CALLAHAN ON THE STRUGGLE FOR ELOQUENCE

Throughout *Invisible Man* Ellison's quest is for eloquence. So is his narrator's. As a writer, Ellison becomes a citizen in the territory of the spoken word while his orator-narrator masters the craft of the written word. Because of the unfinished business of identity and American democracy, the art of eloquence is not simple. At times the pursuit of eloquence calls Invisible Man to think while he is acting and, at others, to act while he is thinking. Eloquence is bound up with persuasion, and, therefore, Invisible Man's eloquence turns on his ability to improvise in genuine response to a situation and an actual audience. . . .

Through his experience as an orator and rabble-rouser, Invisible Man gradually discovers the combination of luck, will, and skill ("shit, grit, and mother-wit" [176]) and the coincidence of self and other required in order for "performance and creation" to merge in a "single, complex act." He is so thoroughly a performer that he defines and tests his identity on those occasions when he becomes a public voice. In his speeches Invisible Man's voice evolves into an instrument more and more keyed to the necessities, limits, and possibilities of call-and-response. To persuade others and move them to action, he relies mostly on techniques of improvisation. Sometimes after the jolt of reversal he learns that his words have consequences dramatically and drastically opposed to his intentions. Several times his speeches lead to unintended actions. For a long time he underestimates the dynamic mutual awareness required between performer and audience for an improvisation to become eloquent. Only gradually—too late for a career as an orator, in time for his new vocation as a writer—does he learn to challenge his audience's skills as well as his own.

Despite his failure to be eloquent with the spoken word, Invisible Man ends up committed to self-reliance as an optimist as well as an ironist. In the novel's paradox, he learns how and why the power of speech can be the power of action only when his potential eloquence falls on closed, Black Nationalist ears during the chaos of a race riot. In time he comes to see eloquence in much the same way as Ellison's literary ancestor and namesake, Ralph Waldo Emerson, understood it. "There is no orator who is not a hero," Emerson declared. "He is challenged and must answer all comers," and his words evoke Invisible Man's struggle for identity through improvisational oratory. But the comparison also breaks down because Invisible Man has been too obsessed with advancing to "the very top" (380) to embody Emerson's heroic conception of eloquence. "The orator's speech," wrote Emerson in the 1840s, when he and others relied on the power of the word to persuade Americans to live out their democratic ideals and free the slaves, "is not to be distinguished from action. *It is the electricity of action.*" Nonetheless, Invisible Man attempts to make Emerson's metaphor work for him. He sends words out like so many charges intended to flow through his audience in a current of action. He misjudges the explosiveness of language and fails as an orator. But later, underground, solitary, and silent, he taps into a literal power line and drains off enough electricity from Monopolated Light and Power to provide light and heat while he generates the energy and symbolic action of his autobiography.

He tells us so in a voice at once brooding and insulting, peremptory and inquiring, in a prologue that is a self-conscious portrait of the artist as a frustrated, failed rabble-rouser. "Whoso would be a man, must be a nonconformist," Emerson wrote in "Self-Reliance." In his prologue Invisible Man does not seek conversation, he can't—not yet. Truly responsive voices might talk back to him, question his motives, undermine his vulnerable, evolving self. Between the prologue and the epilogue, during the twenty-five chapters which tell the story of Invisible Man's life in the world, he fails of eloquence and political leadership because he is so out of touch, so much an isolated, solitary traveler, so much in the grip of illusion (his own and others'), and because he does not yet understand that he and his words are variables in the American equation of power and possibility. Only in the epilogue, having made ironic peace with his identity and his voice, is he ready for response, for conversation, ready to risk verbal acts of intimacy—ready, in short, for eloquence.

Lawrence Jackson on the Concept of Invisibility

One morning, sitting in the open barn, Ellison eased his pen across the paper and wrote out the lines "I am an invisible man." He often doodled on his writing pads, drawing profiles as if still in Eva Hamlin's art class, and playing free-association games. But these words lingered, and haunted him. In a briefcase, he carried an outline, a sheaf of notes and a couple of typed pages of the novel he had been working on. His hero was a sentient young black pilot who had, the mixed fortune to outrank all of the other American officers at a German prison camp. He was even reading Lord Raglan's *The Hero* as research to help him structure the mythic dimensions of his character. But despite the appealing heroism of his character and the timeliness of a war story (Ellison had noted young private Norman Mailer's long story, which became *The Naked and the Dead*), the lines he had just written about invisibility, and the dilemma of existence as a black American, wormed their way into him. Within a couple of days he had the germ of a story, one that resonated most deeply for him, in part because it was his own.

Ellison had encountered the idea of invisibility that summer while reading James Joyce to prepare a lecture that Stanley Hyman had invited him to give at Bennington College, where Hyman had recently gained an appointment. In *Ulysses*, when Stephen Daedelus thinks of his mother, he imagines her hearing a pantomime of *Turko the Terrible*. "I am the boy / That can enjoy / Invisibility."[30] The idea he had encountered in Joyce and the prospect of creating the "uncreated conscience" of his race, combined with the tranquillity he enjoyed in the Green Mountains of Vermont, prompted Ellison to hear and respond to an insistent and demanding fictional voice.

A vault of charged emotions was opened when Ellison embraced the theme of his masterwork. He experienced a cathartic moment, in which he could safely divulge the deep-seated pain that he had carried with him over the years. Dramatic scenes crept into his mind that summer, homegrown and rooted in Ellison's most trying personal moments, in Oklahoma City and at Tuskegee. As was his tendency, he recalled the most poignant and painful memories with humor and irony. He remembered having dogs set upon him walking down the roads—the spectacles, insults, and burlesques of a poor black teenager's life in Oklahoma City. He recalled the dangers he faced onboard the train to college and the violence that almost incapacitated him for his music school audition. He thought most bitterly of losing his scholarship and the charades he endured in the campus Chapel.

Writing the earliest chapters of the novel that bubbled out of him, Ellison could derive satisfaction from the sense that his work was markedly different from Wright's. Although his theme was similar to Wright's, particularly in Wright's *Black Boy* and "The Man Who Lived Underground"—the journey of a black male toward self-conscious possession of his identity in a hostile or indifferent world—Ellison's approach was unique. His work did not necessarily confine itself to protest or struggle, but instead, exaggerated and made spectacular the conjunctions of black and white life, always tuning to a fine pitch the distinction between the misery and the comedy of these episodes. Blending elements of the comic, the tragic, and the absurd, he made it impossible to simply pity the protagonist, and subsequently increased the reader's ability to see beyond racial identity. The narrator was already making his entrance as an ambitious and bright college boy, capable, at points at least, of recognizing and articulating his conundrum. In fact, the narrator was so bright that he would erase Ellison's personal shame; instead of graduating high school at twenty, the narrator is a college junior at nineteen.

The development of the outline occurred fairly rapidly, though it would take Ellison roughly six years to complete the novel, which became his most significant work. After a year he had outlined the first half of the project, and before the end of 1947 he had a fairly coherent idea of how the story should end. Before the end of 1945, he had sketched out versions of the first section, in which an underhanded college president named Bledsoe expels the hero from school. Ellison chose to explore the contradiction of black identity, the idea of a competing and opposite reality that is submerged but rides alongside of popularly recognized poses of existence. The humble Bledsoe was a tyrant; the hero's accommodating grandfather a revolutionary. Here was part of the twelve-toned musical scale he hoped to use in his fictional orchestrations. In Wright's *Black Boy*, the protagonist says, "Negroes too sometimes have those dreams," an understatement that ironically suggests the common humanity of blacks and whites. Ellison took the next step, the assumption of shared dreams among black and white, and made his hero's quest an unflagging pursuit of individual discovery. The strategy was a gamble in an anti-black world.

Note

30. James Joyce, *Ulysses* (1922; New York: Random House, 1934): 9, line 1.259–261.

Shelly Eversley on Female Invisibility in the Novel

In 1953, one year after the publication of Ralph Ellison's *Invisible Man*, Hugh Hefner launched his men's magazine, *Playboy*. The magazine's centerfold featured a nude Marilyn Monroe posed against a striking red velvet curtain. The photograph was taken in 1949 as Ellison was working diligently on the novel, and it became a quintessential example of American femininity, an icon of American cultural history. As a photographer, art student, and collector of painting and portraiture, Ellison understood the power of visual images. . . .

Vision is perhaps the most underexplored aspect of *Invisible Man*. More than a literal question of seeing, the protagonist's life depends on his ability to "learn to look beneath the surface" and discern reality despite "mirrors of hard, distorting glass" (153, 3). Such discernment requires he learn to distinguish salient meaning from stereotype. While critics have discussed the phenomenological implications of Invisible Man's desire to be seen, his desire for social equality, few engage the contradictory significance of what he sees, and more importantly, how he processes the visual image. . . .

At the Battle Royal and in his "blind terror" (21), a metaphor of proliferating invisibility, invisible man sees only the image of a "magnificent blonde," her image constructed in the social imaginary. While he has not yet developed insight, he begins to learn its lessons. In this scene that frames the entire novel, the woman—also nameless and "stark naked"—stands before the protagonist, the fearful black boys, and the town's most respected white men. The novel's description frames her visually, and her subjectivity first appears through the male eyes that look at her body. Her humanity seems to disappear as her body submits to the voyeuristic gaze that renders her a pornographic sex object. She is invisible. Her manipulated image presents stereotypes of truth and social authority that rationalize domination over women and black people. For the narrator, however, this woman prompts him to see and feel ambivalence: "I wanted at one and the same time to caress her and destroy her, to love her and murder her, to hide from her, and yet to stroke where below the small American flag tattooed on her belly her thighs formed a capital V" (19). Even as the woman's presence provokes a visceral response, the protagonist's engagement calls attention to her visual and revelatory significance. For instance, the V of the woman's thighs juxtaposed with the American flag signals democratic victory. As Ellison began writing *Invisible Man* at the end of World War II, the United States had defeated totalitarian threats against global humanity. This victory not only positioned the nation as the world's leading democracy, it also promised integration, an honest racial equality that would finally realize the most sacred principles of American freedom. Yet, at the same time, the V between the woman's thighs also represents her gender difference and it reminds the protagonist of women's unequal status. Looking past the symbolic surface of the "magnificent blonde," Invisible Man begins to realize that no victory has been won. Neither the woman nor the man can rely on the national symbols that should, in actuality, indicate their freedoms.

In the segregated United States, a black man's gaze upon a white woman could, in the South, warrant death by lynching. By accepting the risk associated with the deathly potential of looking at a white woman ("[h]ad the price of looking been blindness, I would have looked," he says), invisible man refuses the tyranny of monopolated vision. He rebels against the social order that objectifies him and the woman in order to rethink the unreality that shrouds her appearance. The protagonist looks: "she began to dance . . . the smoke of a hundred cigars clinging to her like the thinnest of veils." The veils and the smoke imagistically emphasize the blinders that make her invisibility possible, and then they invoke another myth, Salome, whose seemingly promiscuous sexuality conceals her gender oppression. Salome's sensual dance allegedly cost John the Baptist his life. But, like the multiple meanings of the V between the blond woman's thighs, Salome's reluctant dance suggests more. In the myth, Salome refuses the persistent and inappropriate sexual advances of the King, her stepfather. Like "the most important men of [invisible man's] town," the king demands that Salome dance. In an act meant to demonstrate his masculine authority, his offer to compensate her for her services is calculated to reduce an independent woman to a possession, as one to be purchased as one would a whore.[11] The parallel between Salome's "Dance of the Seven Veils" and the blond woman's dance calls attention to the links between the myth of a dangerous, forbidden female sexuality and a blind-sighted objectification of women. Salome, like "the magnificent blonde," only *appears* to possess a dangerously seductive power over men.

A chauvinistic power that subjugates women and people of color distorts the protagonist's vision, for in his blindness he mistakes the blonde as a threat to his progress. As invisible man looks at "the magnificent blonde," he sees yet another myth:

"She seemed like a fair bird-girl girdled in veils calling to me from the angry surface of some gray and threatening sea" (19). This Homeric and Joycean image invokes a siren, a nymph, part bird and part woman, who lures sailors to their death with her seductive singing. When he finally sees the woman distinct from her mythic sexuality—"I saw the terror and disgust in her eyes, almost like my own terror and that which I saw in the others boys"—he begins to understand their shared subjugation (20). The novel offers no pause, no distinction, between the woman's dance as pornographic entertainment and the boys' fight, the Battle Royal, that immediately follows. This seamlessness depicts their common position in relation to a social authority that falsely constructs their positions as opposites. As the protagonist describes the chaos and the terror of his own fight, like "a joggled camera sweeps in a reeling scene," he reminds the reader of its visual and symbolic resonance. He narrates chromatically—"The room went red as I fell"—and invisible man invites the reader to see, with "inner eyes," the importance of his struggle in relation to women who, shrouded in myth, also struggle with the burden of invisibility (20). Invisible man's red room predicts retribution and earth shattering revelation, as does the ominous red moon that is present in the Salome myth.[12]

The narrator's blindness and his insight in relation to the blonde woman initiates his education in invisibility. As he becomes aware of the distinction between formal education and the kind of knowledge that affords insight, invisible man recalls the images that inspire his illumination. He wonders whether the statue of the College Founder presents a "witnessing of revelation or a more efficient blinding," and in his resistance to blindness he becomes an intellectual. His "mind's eye" demands that he seek answers to his questions, "Why? And how? How and why?" (36).

Notes

11. In the New Testament, Salome is the daughter of Queen Herodias and step-daughter to King Herod Antipas. John the Baptist condemns Salome's mother's marriage to Herod, her first husband's brother. Herod holds John the Baptist prisoner, but he is afraid to

kill him since many think John a man of God. Herod also lusts for his young stepdaughter, so on his birthday he asks her to dance for him. She declines; but, when Herod offers her *anything* in his kingdom in exchange for the dance, she accepts. Upon concluding her seductive dance, "The Dance of the Seven Veils," she asks for John the Baptist's head delivered to her. Fearfully and reluctantly, Herod honors her wish, and Salome delivers the head to her mother. See Mark 6:14–29. For centuries many have represented Salome as the original femme fatale, a symbol of the erotic and dangerous woman. See paintings such as "The Dance of Salome" by Benozzo Gozzoli (c. 1461–81), and "Salome with the Head of John the Baptist" by Carlo Dola (c. 1600). Oscar Wilde's controversial one act tragedy (first published in 1893), suggests that Herod's lascivious looks and his sexual desire for his stepdaughter, coupled with Iokanaan's (John the Baptist's) scorn for Salome and her mother ("By women came evil into this world" [22]), position Salome as the subject and object of a more general masculine contempt for women. See Aubrey Beardsley and Oscar Wilde, *Salome: A Tragedy in One Act* (New York: Dover Publications, 1967). German composer Richard Strauss was so moved by Wilde's account of Salome (who is unnamed in the biblical story), that he composed the opera, *Salome*, first performed in Dresden in 1905.

12. In Wilde's account of Salome's story, Iokanaan's death also marks the appearance of a blood red moon. In the Bible, a red moon represents the realization of the prophecy of Revelation: "the moon turned red as blood all over, and the stars of the sky fell onto the earth . . . For the Great Day of his retribution has come . . ." See Revelation 6:12–7.

Ross Posnock Compares the Political Views of Ralph Ellison and Hannah Arendt

Ellison's 1952 novel constructs the political in ways that bear striking comparison with Arendt's epochal redescription of the political six years later in *The Human Condition* (1958). Bringing these texts together may at first seem anomalous, not least because in the 1960s they enjoyed nearly antithetical reputations among those on the left. Arendt's book, along with her *On Revolution* of 1963, inspired some in the civil rights struggle and especially those in the Free Speech Movement in Berkeley[10]. Like many of the intellectual leaders of the New Left, Arendt rejected both Marxism (for its fetish of labor and its determinism) and liberalism (for its valorizing of the private and minimizing of politics). She insisted on the possibility of recovering human action in the face of the increasing "world alienation" characteristic of modernity—man's withdrawal from the public realm, a retreat underwritten by equating freedom with freedom from politics[11]. . . .

As a prime example of "world alienation" one might easily nominate Ellison's protagonist domiciled underground where, after nearly 600 pages, he reluctantly concludes that he has "overstayed" his "hibernation" (*Invisible* 581). By the late 1960s many readers had lost patience with such a (seemingly) temporizing stance; black nationalists held Ellison's novel up to scorn, condemning it as quietist and elitist. Reading Ellison and Arendt together helps recover not only the complicated status of hibernation—that, as Ellison's narrator notes early on, "hibernation is a covert preparation for a more overt action"—but foregrounds what readers often ignore: the catalytic effect upon the narrator of witnessing the "overt action" of a group in Harlem acting in concert to end inhuman living conditions (*Invisible* 13). Seeing near the novel's end this organized collective "capable of their own action" inspires his fragile hope that until the "world" is put in a "strait-jacket, its definition is possibility" (548, 576).

Ellison, like Arendt, reanimated the possibility of political participation during a postwar period when the very notion of meaningful agency had been cast into doubt by the trauma of totalitarianism. A flight from politics into the consolations of self-cultivation became one response among intellectuals to Nazism and Stalinism, some justifying it by believing that "an end to ideology" (in Daniel Bell's famous phrase) was imminent with the Allied victory. . . .

What are the obstacles to the creative action of politics? Invisible Man offers a clue when he affirms in the prologue his belief in action "despite Brother Jack and all that sad, lost period of the Brotherhood" (*Invisible* 13). In opposing "action" to the political activism of Brotherhood, Ellison posits a tacit distinction that deserves explicit articulation. What Ellison keeps tacit here becomes a major chord later in the novel—how

Brotherhood's scientistic logic of historical inevitability ("we are champions of a scientific approach to society") and its mantra of discipline and sacrifice smother the contingency and spontaneity of actual political action—and hence its very creativity—by harnessing it to an absolute called History (with a capital H). This word is one that members of Brotherhood (another inert slogan) endlessly intone as if they control it as one would "a force in a laboratory experiment" (*Invisible* 441). Marxism's necessitarianism, expressed, for instance, in Brother Jack's casual remark that "individuals don't count" for they are "incapable of rising to the necessity of the historical situation" (291) paradoxically makes its political goals profoundly anti-political in the Ellisonian and Arendtian sense.

This discovery repeatedly crystallizes for Invisible Man late in the novel, first in the epiphanies he has in the aftermath of Tod Clifton's death about those "men of transition" "too obscure for learned classification," who "plunge" "outside the groove of history," and then in his participation in the Harlem riot near the novel's close (439, 440, 443). During this latter episode, the narrator stumbles upon a group of men, led by the compelling, taciturn Dupre. The group is bent on "fixing to do something that needs to be done" and to do it with organization and the right tools (542). After getting flashlights and buckets of oil, Dupre and his men carefully soak their despised "deathtrap" of a tenement with kerosene, empty the building of tenants and then calmly, methodically, torch it: "my kid died from the t-bees" in there, remarks Dupre as the flames begin to leap (547). Observing Dupre's determined actions on behalf of community renewal, invisible man recognizes a new kind of leader: "he was a type of man nothing in my life has taught me to see, to understand, or respect, a man outside the scheme till now . . . What would Brother Jack say of him?" (547).

What makes Dupre unprecedented is his redemption of the "insult of oblivion" (to borrow Arendt's phrase), an act that places him outside the "futile game of 'making history'" where one is merely a pawn in the hands of white power brokers (575). Instead of making history, i.e., assimilating to

Brotherhood's grand narrative, Dupre emerges as a political actor whose speech and deeds bring into being a collective intervention, unveiling the "web of human relationships" latent in the sufferings of those in the Harlem tenement (*Human* 163). This disclosure exhilarates the narrator: "I was seized with a fierce sense of exaltation. They've done it, I thought. They organized it and carried it through alone; the decision their own and their own action. Capable of their own action" (*Invisible* 548). This action gives birth to the possibility of something new—the destruction of dehumanizing conditions. The fire not only opens a space for change, long promised but never delivered by Brotherhood, but renounces the passive, private suffering that is the lot of the invisible—those "excluded from the light of the public realm" (*Revolution* 69).

Notes

10. See *Seeds of the Sixties*, A. Jamison and R. Eyerman (Berkeley CA: University of California Press, 1993), p. 53.

11. Hannah Arendt, *The Human Condition* (New York, Doubleday Anchor, 1958), p. 231; *Men in Dark Times* (Harmondsworth: Pelican, 1975), p. 12.

Anne Anlin Cheng on Ambiguity in Racial Encounters

In the Prologue to Ralph Ellison's *Invisible Man*, the narrator explicates the novel's central metaphor by telling us that he is invisible because "[white] people refuse to see [him]."[1] The narrator proceeds to illustrate this assertion with a story about a violent confrontation that took place between himself and a white man:

> One night I accidentally bumped into a man . . . he looked insolently out of his blue eyes and cursed me . . . I yelled, "Apologize! Apologize!" But he continued to curse and struggle, and I butted him again and again until he went down heavily . . . I kicked him profusely . . . when it

> occurred to me that the man had not *seen* me, actually; that he, as far as he knew, was walking in midst of a walking nightmare . . . a man almost killed by a phantom. (4)

This passage offers a striking yet enigmatic vision of the nature of racial blindness. Seemingly explicit, the description nonetheless opens up layers of complicated questions about the differences between perception and projection, between action and reaction, in a racial encounter. From the narrator's perspective, we see the white man's "insolence" as anger from having to confront what he presumably did not want to see. The white man's curse, upon being bumped, expresses a wish to deny the black man who is no longer "invisible" and who is now actively demanding his right of way. The white man's resistance to this presence reminds us that "black invisibility" grows out of dominant culture's privilege to see or to not see, a privilege substantiated by a history of longstanding material, legal, and social discrimination. The metaphor of invisibility thus alerts us to the repercussions of this long process of social and legal exclusion.

At the same time, when we attend to Ellison's description more fully, we have to ask: is the white man the only one suffering from blindness in this scene? The writing is ambiguous. Who is the invisible one? If the narrator bumps into the white man, is not the white man the one who is invisible to the black man? The narrator bumps into what *he* did not see and then accuses the other of blindness. If we do not take the narrator's account at its surface value, it is conceivable that the white man cursed the black man for his clumsiness rather than for racist reasons, that masculine rather than racial privilege may be at stake, and that the narrator's detection of the white man's insolence may itself be a projection growing out of the former's own self-denigration and wounded pride in the face of "blue eyes," a historically incendiary sign for whiteness.

This ambiguous scenario highlights the fraught consequences of the history of racism for both dominant and minority cultures. The point here is not to discount the invisible man's interpretation of the event, nor to dismiss the possibility of racism at work. The issue is, more crucially, the realization that because of the historic relation between whites and blacks in this country the possibility of a rac*ist* response haunts every potentially rac*ial* encounter. A pre-written script compels, if not dictates, this confrontation. In this loaded exchange, mutual invisibility as the result of mutual projection seems unavoidable. Indeed, the incident becomes a racial one, not because a black man and a white man are involved per se, but because of the overdetermined history between them.

The insight that invisibility rarely presents a one-sided projection poses a challenging notion for a liberal politics dedicated to social progress and the amelioration of racism and racist effects. For Ellison's careful composition of the encounter above suggests that one of the most insidious effects of discrimination may be that it perpetuates itself, even on the part of the discriminated. "Racial injury" thus alludes to a fraught nexus of implications that revolve around psychical as well as material effects. More than fifty years after the publication of *Invisible Man*, the issue of racial injury and its effects continue to present a central problem for civil progress. On the one hand, progressive politics criticize the perspective that racism has wreaked psychical damage on racial minorities for its potential to re-victimize these individuals. (That is, it can be damaging to say how damaging racism has been.) On the one hand, there is wide agreement that the discourse of racial injury has played a key role in promoting civil rights reform during the past half century. The task of acknowledging the grief of racial injury without denying or sentimentalizing its legacy presents a central challenge for contemporary politics. Recent debates over the polemics of reparation, for instance, highlight the complexities haunting the issue of racial damage and compensation. While institutional recognition of historic wrongs (in the forms of monetary and/or symbolic acknowledgments) are important, it also raises a host of ethical and pragmatic questions: does material compensation absolve ethical responsibility? How much compensation is enough? How, indeed, does one *quantify* injury? With its bold explorations of the double binds that structure the effects of racism on the discriminated, *Invisible Man* remains remarkably germane at the beginning of the twenty-first century as we continue to scrutinize the meanings of multiculturalism and pluralism.

Note

1. Ralph Ellison, *Invisible Man* (New York: Vintage Books, 1990), p. 3.

Michael Anderson on Ellison's Failed Genius

Ralph Ellison and alienation: It would seem an obvious pairing. After all, he won his initial acclaim for extending the most fashionable affectation of the 1950s onto black America. Yet he may be better remembered (more esteemed, certainly, in certain circles) for his strenuous advocacy of inclusion, association, interconnection. The paradox is but one of many in a man for whom paradox too often has been mistaken for profundity: a writer who did not write, the expositor of "complexity" whose ideas were simple when not simplistic, the delineator of "chaos" whose commentary was a compendium of complacency, the advocate of social fluidity whose vision was frozen in times past, the proponent of aesthetic discipline whose work is marked by formlessness and lack of control, a "race man" who disdained his race, the critic of sociology whose own novel has been distorted into a sociological cliché, the proponent of individualism whose career was propelled at every step by an astonishing array of selfless supporters, an artist all the more honored the less he produced, a public presence as an invisible man. . . .

Ellison's protagonist, with his giddy naïveté, psychological shallowness and sketchy background, is the least representative black figure in American literature. . . . In fact, one of the novel's major flaws is that Ellison's black Candide suddenly shows signs of flesh and blood once he becomes involved in the Brotherhood; the prose loses its ironic lightness and assumes shades of anguish ("At what point do we stop? Is this the new definition, is Brotherhood a matter of sacrificing the weak? If so, at what point do we stop?") and despair ("Only in the Brotherhood had there seemed a chance for such as us, the mere glimmer of a light. . . . And even that was without meaning"). It is not until he feels betrayed by the Brotherhood that he declares himself invisible, "invisible," as Rampersad points out, "to everyone, black or white."

In his astute commentary on *Invisible Man*, Rampersad, who teaches English and the humanities at Stanford, notes Ellison's technical mistake: "He gives the Brotherhood no plausible reason for deserting the cause of black rights." In life, of course, it was because the Nazi invasion of the Soviet Union caused the party to sacrifice black rights in favor of American war efficiency. . . .

The party opposed A. Philip Randolph's proposed March on Washington, the Rubicon for Ellison and many other blacks—though he would publish "ultra-Marxist criticism under a pseudonym even as he was abandoning the radical left." Editors at *New Masses* told Ellison to "soft-pedal this Negro thing. We've got to get production going." Perhaps to placate him, the magazine also started paying him for his articles; as Rampersad notes, "Ralph and black intellectuals like him were more important than ever." Conspicuous in its absence, the sense of racial betrayal—"If only we had some true friends, some who saw us as more than convenient tools for shaping their own desires!"—makes *Invisible Man* a document of black anti-Communist disillusionment. . . .

"A crisis of spirit and technique haunts [the] last section" of *Invisible Man*, Rampersad writes. "The book was not finished. Ralph needed to add something in order to reassert a final measure of control over his epic." The novel's epilogue imposes a meaning not justified by what precedes it; Rampersad joins a host of previous commentators in pointing out how undefined are the "infinite possibilities" the *Invisible Man* claims for himself. How could they be? This lack of definition was what Ellison called "complexity." . . . Yet for Ellison "complexity" was the flip side of "chaos." It was where he found his creative freedom—as he wrote of Rinehart, "His world was possibility and he knew it. He was years ahead of me and I was a fool"—yet it also carried his deepest emotional danger: "Creative experience," he wrote to Albert Murray, brought "only a fighting chance with the chaos of living."

A final paradox: In the end Ralph Ellison was alienated even from the wellspring of his creativity. His muse pulled him toward the sort of creation . . . his will and his psyche would not permit him to sustain. Though the sections of *Invisible Man* dealing with the Brotherhood are the most emotionally felt, the ones with the greatest artistic power—Trueblood with his ribald tale of incest, the mental patients in the Golden Day, the nightmarish Harlem riot—describe a world gone mad. Norman Mailer, in his notorious "Quick and Expensive Comments" on his fellow writers, hit a bull's-eye when he judged that "Ellison's mind, fine and icy, tuned to the pitch of a major novelist's madness, is not always adequate to mastering the forms of rage, horror, and disgust which his eyes have presented to his experience, and so he is forever tumbling from the heights of pure satire into the nets of a murderously depressed clown." That Ellison was not fitted for the art he professed to admire is his pathos. He sought to be the black T.S. Eliot when he could have been the black Beckett.

Works by Ralph Ellison

Invisible Man, 1952

The Writer's Experience (with Karl Shapiro), 1964

Shadow and Act, 1964

The City in Crisis (with Whitney M. Young, Jr., and Herbert Gans), 1967

Going to the Territory, 1986

Juneteenth, 1999

Annotated Bibliography

Benston, Kimberly W., ed. *Speaking for You: The Vision of Ralph Ellison*. Washington, DC: Howard University Press, 1987.

Speaking for You takes its title from the last line of *Invisible Man* to emphasize what its author believes is the singular achievement of Ralph Ellison—his ability to bring together the cultural, political, and personal. He states in his introduction that the choice of essays was made explicitly to illuminate this unified and unifying vision.

Busby, Mark. *Ralph Ellison*. Boston: Twayne Publishers, 1991.

Mark Busby's work on Ellison is part of the Twayne series on writers. It is intended as an introduction to the life and work of Ellison and is especially helpful outlining the literary influences that inspired Ellison. A brief chronology is included.

Callahan, John F., ed. *Ralph Ellison's "Invisible Man": A Casebook*. Oxford: Oxford University Press, 2004.

Editor John Callahan takes a long (fifty year) look at *Invisible Man* and its ongoing power and relevance. In addition to commentary by recognized students and critics of the novel, Callahan includes substantial commentary by Ellison himself. Many have noted that as an author Ellison was unusually forthcoming about his own book, willingly participating in public and private discussions of its origins, long view, and individual episodes.

Hersey, John, ed. *Ralph Ellison: A Collection of Critical Essays*. Englewood Cliffs, NJ: Prentice-Hall, Inc., 1974.

This collection includes essays by prominent critics like Saul Bellow, Robert Penn Warren, Irving Howe, and Tony Tanner. The introduction consists mainly of a conversation presented as an interview that editor Hersey had with Ellison who, with his wife, was a weekend guest.

Jackson, Lawrence. *Ralph Ellison: Emergence of Genius*. New York: John Wiley & Sons, Inc., 2002.

This recent and lengthy biography of Ellison begins with the earliest influences of family and hometown and travels with him to Tuskegee and then to New York City and public acclaim and controversy. Much information is included about Ellison's association with leftist intellectuals active in political issues from the 1920s through the 1940s, including the Communist Party of America. It was through the party that Ellison found an eager receptivity to his work and his first opportunities for becoming a published writer. The party, however, while remarkably and authentically free of racial prejudices, had no use for Ellison's growing emphasis on artistic accomplishment over class struggle from the Marxist perspective. Jackson includes many details of the history of these clashes between the artistic and ideological perspectives.

McSweeney, Kerry. *Invisible Man: Race and Identity*. Boston: Twayne Publishers, 1988.

Kerry McSweeney's book is another of the useful introductions to Ralph Ellison. It offers a chapter-by-chapter analysis of *Invisible Man*, a chronology, and some information about the novel's critical reception.

Murray, Albert and John F. Callahan, eds. *Trading Twelves: The Selected Letters of Ralph Ellison and Albert Murray*. New York: The Modern Library, 2000.

Trading Twelves is an exchange of letters written during the 1950s between Ellison and Albert Murray who met as students at Tuskegee. Murray, also an aspiring but unpublished writer, was teaching at Tuskegee where Ellison, a published and acclaimed writer, was a "dropout." Despite this difference in status, the two were not diminished by small rivalries; rather, they sought out and measured each other's insights. An exchange of thoughts about Ellison's sojourn to Rome is included.

Nadel, Alan. *Invisible Criticism: Ralph Ellison and the American Canon*. Iowa City: University of Iowa Press, 1988.

What gets read (the official canon) is akin, according to Alan Nadel, to what gets seen and heard (political power). Nadel uses the "invisibility" theme to look admiringly at the way Ellison interacted with and made use of the canonical writers preceding him, and by this interaction rearranging our perspectives on them. The chapter comparing Invisible Man with Mark Twain's Huck and Jim is especially entertaining and insightful.

O'Meally, Robert G. *The Craft of Ralph Ellison*. Cambridge and London: Harvard University Press, 1980.

This study focuses on a theme of singular importance to Ellison, the man and the writer: the development of individual consciousness as a necessary step toward personal freedom. This stand brought controversy to *Invisible Man* and to Ellison's own life, with competing voices arguing that major reforms in the distribution of political power had to come before individual freedom. Since Ellison insisted that black history was indelibly and indisputably a part of American history—in contrast to the Black Separatist Movement—O'Meally provides a good picture of the black and slave folklore, legend, and artistic expression that Ellison made a major component of *Invisible Man*.

Parr, Susan Resneck and Pancho Savery, eds. *Approaches to Teaching Ellison's "Invisible Man."* New York: The Modern Language Association of America, 1989.

The *Approaches to Teaching* series takes into account the diversity of students reading a particular work and aims to cover all the relevant perspectives. While especially useful for teachers, this book offers far-ranging information and analysis for the general reader as well. For the study of *Invisible Man*, topics include minority writers, perspectives for inner city schools, and ethnicity. Resources for further research and suggested methods for teaching the novel to different populations are included.

Posnock, Ross, ed. *The Cambridge Companion to Ralph Ellison*. Cambridge: Cambridge University Press, 2005.

The Cambridge Companion series consistently offers stimulating and insightful commentary. Editor Ross Posnock writes in his introduction that one purpose of this collection of essays will be to "... unsettle received wisdom [about Ellison] particularly the various static images affixed to [him] over the decades" (2).

Sundquist, Eric J. *Cultural Contexts for Ralph Ellison's "Invisible Man."* Boston: Bedford Books of St. Martin's Press, 1995.

Sundquist gathered the materials for this book to provide an historical and cultural context for understanding Ellison's novel. Few novels, he asserts, have such an extensive range of references; students coming to *Invisible Man* for the first or tenth time will find in this collection details from American legal and literary history, African American cultural memory, and references to Western culture in general. Emphasis is put on African American materials because these have been less available to the general reader. This book is fascinating in its own right but invaluable for understanding the depth and intensity behind Ellison's achievement.

Watts, Jerry Gafio. *Heroism and the Black Intellectual: Ralph Ellison, Politics, and Afro-American Intellectual Life*. Chapel Hill and London: University of North Carolina Press, 1994.

This erudite and engaging book on Ellison is especially useful for readers interested in contemporary African American studies, in particular the contributions of black intellectuals like Ellison himself. The old but still-relevant issues of political protest versus artistic achievement are especially interestingly discussed. One example, perhaps not widely known, describes Ellison's negative reaction to the poet Robert Lowell's refusal to attend a White House celebration of contemporary artists to protest President Johnson's waging of the Vietnam War. Prominent thinkers currently active in American cultural life are listed as inspiring voices behind Watts's work—Cornell West and Henry Louis Gates among them.

Contributors

Harold Bloom is Sterling Professor of the Humanities at Yale University. He is the author of 30 books, including *Shelley's Mythmaking*, *The Visionary Company*, *Blake's Apocalypse*, *Yeats*, *A Map of Misreading*, *Kabbalah and Criticism*, *Agon: Toward a Theory of Revisionism*, *The American Religion*, *The Western Canon*, and *Omens of Millennium: The Gnosis of Angels, Dreams, and Resurrection*. *The Anxiety of Influence* sets forth Professor Bloom's provocative theory of the literary relationships between the great writers and their predecessors. His most recent books include *Shakespeare: The Invention of the Human*, a 1998 National Book Award finalist, *How to Read and Why*, *Genius: A Mosaic of One Hundred Exemplary Creative Minds*, *Hamlet: Poem Unlimited*, *Where Shall Wisdom Be Found?*, and *Jesus and Yahweh: The Names Divine*. In 1999, Professor Bloom received the prestigious American Academy of Arts and Letters Gold Medal for Criticism. He has also received the International Prize of Catalonia, the Alfonso Reyes Prize of Mexico, and the Hans Christian Andersen Bicentennial Prize of Denmark.

Ralph Ellison is the author of *The Invisible Man* (1952), *Shadow and Act* (1964), and *Going to the Territory* (1986). His *Collected Essays* (1995), and the novel fragment *Juneteenth* (1999) were published posthumously.

Larry Neal is a poet and one of the founders of the Black Arts Movement. He is the author of *Black Boogaloo* and coeditor of *Black Fire: An Anthology of Afro-American Writing*.

Kerry McSweeney is the author of *Tennyson and Swinburne as Romantic Naturalists* (1981), *Four Contemporary Novelists* (1983), and *George Eliot: A Literary Life* (1991).

Alan Nadel taught literature at Rensselaer Polytechnic Institute. In 1988 he won the Margaret Church-MFS Memorial Award for his essay on Alice Walker.

Walter Slatoff taught English at Cornell University.

Eric J. Sundquist is Professor of English at the University of California at Los Angeles. He is the author of *To Wake the Nations: Race in the Making of American Literature* (1993).

John F. Callahan is Morgan S. Odell Professor of Humanities at Lewis and Clark College.

Lawrence Jackson teaches English at Emory University.

Shelly Eversley teaches English at Baruch College, CUNY. Her essays have been published in *American Literary History* and *Minnesota Review.*

Ross Posnock teaches English at Columbia University. He is the author of *Color and Culture: Black Writers and the Making of the Modern Intellectual* (1998).

Anne Anlin Cheng teaches English at the University of California at Berkeley. She is the author of *The Melancholy of Race* (2000).

Michael Anderson writes for *The Nation*; he is currently working on a biography of the playwright Lorraine Hansberry.

Acknowledgments

Ellison, Ralph. From "On Initiation Rites and Power," *Ralph Ellison's Invisible Man: A Casebook*, p. 343. © 2004 by Oxford University Press.

Neal, Larry. From "Ellison's Zoot Suit," *Ralph Ellison: A Collection of Critical Essays*, pp. 70–72, 78–79. © 1974 by Prentice-Hall, Inc.

From *Invisible Man: Race and Identity* by Kerry McSweeney. 1998. Reprinted with permission of Thomson Learning: www.thomsonrights.com. Fax 800 730-2215.

Nadel, Alan. From "Invisible Man, Huck, and Jim." Reprinted from *Invisible Criticism: Ralph Ellison and the American Canon*, by the University of Iowa Press, 1988.

Reprinted by permission of the Modern Language Association of America. From Walter Slatoff, "Making Invisible Man Matter," *Approaches to Teaching Ellison's Invisible Man*, edited by Susan Resneck Parr and Pancho Savery, MLA, 1989.

From *Cultural Contexts for Ralph Ellison's Invisible Man* by Eric J. Sundquist. Copyright © 2/95 by Bedford/St. Martin's. Reproduced by permission of Bedford/St. Martin's.

Callahan, John F. From "Ellison's *Invisible Man*," *Ralph Ellison's Invisible Man: A Casebook*, pp. 302, 304–305. © 2004 by Oxford University Press.

Jackson, Lawrence. From *Ralph Ellison: Emergence of Genius*, pp. 320–321. © 2002 by Lawrence Jackson.

Eversley, Shelly. "Female Iconograhy in Invisible Man," *The Cambridge Companion to Ralph Ellison*, edited by Ross Posnock, 2005.

Posnock, Ross. "Ellison, Arendt and the Meaning of Politics," *The Cambridge Companion to Ralph Ellison*, edited by Ross Posnock, 2005.

Cheng, Anne Anlin. "Ralph Ellison and the Politics of Melancholia," *The Cambridge Companion to Ralph Ellison*, edited by Ross Posnock, 2005.

Anderson, Michael. From "At a Loss for Words." *The Nation*, May 28, 2007, pp. 11, 14, 17–18.

Index

Characters in literary works are indexed by first name (if any), followed by the name of the work in parentheses